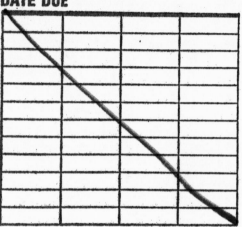

Critical Periods of History

ROBERT D. CROSS, GENERAL EDITOR

Books now in print:

LINCOLN AND THE FIRST SHOT
BY RICHARD N. CURRENT

THE ELECTION OF ANDREW JACKSON
BY ROBERT V. REMINI

McKINLEY, BRYAN, AND THE PEOPLE
BY PAUL W. GLAD

WHY LENIN? WHY STALIN?
A Reappraisal of the Russian Revolution, 1900–1930
BY THEODORE H. VON LAUE

THE LONG FUSE
An Interpretation of the Origins of World War I
BY LAURENCE LAFORE

LABOR IN CRISIS
The Steel Strike of 1919
BY DAVID BRODY

IRISH-AMERICAN NATIONALISM, 1870–1890
BY THOMAS N. BROWN

THOMAS N. BROWN

IRISH-AMERICAN
NATIONALISM
1870-1890

CRITICAL PERIODS OF HISTORY

J. B. Lippincott Company

PHILADELPHIA & NEW YORK

To Mary:
Who Knows the Story

September 1913

What need you, being come to sense
But fumble in a greasy till
And add the halfpence to the pence
And prayer to shivering prayer, until
You have dried the marrow from the bone;
For men were born to pray and save;
Romantic Ireland's dead and gone,
It's with O'Leary in the grave.

Yet they were of a different kind,
The names that stilled your childish play,
They have gone about the world like wind,
But little time had they to pray
For whom the hangman's rope was spun,
And what, God help us, could they save?
Romantic Ireland's dead and gone,
It's with O'Leary in the grave.

Was it for this the wild geese spread
The grey wing upon every tide;
For this that all that blood was shed,
For this Edward Fitzgerald died,
And Robert Emmet and Wolfe Tone,
All that delirium of the brave?
Romantic Ireland's dead and gone,
It's with O'Leary in the grave.

❀   ❀   ❀   ❀   ❀   ❀   ❀

WILLIAM BUTLER YEATS

Acknowledgments

Many persons have aided and encouraged me in the writing of this book. Professor Moses Rischin of San Francisco State College, patron of Irish-American studies, and Mr. Owen Edwards of the University of Oregon read the work in manuscript and saved me from many blunders. Professor John V. Kelleher of Harvard University has over the years shaped my understanding of Irish and Irish-American affairs by his own incomparable knowledge. To Professor Oscar Handlin of Harvard University, under whose direction this study was originally begun as a doctoral dissertation, I am indebted for whatever understanding I have of the role of the immigrant in American life. Professor T. W. Moody of Trinity College, Dublin, Professor R. Dudley Edwards of University College, Dublin, and Professor Lawrence J. McCaffrey of Marquette University critically appraised my approach to the New Departure. Miss Helen Landreth of the Irish Library, Boston College, and the Reverend Thomas T. McAvoy of the University of Notre Dame Archives were more than generous in making available materials in their libraries. To the American Philosophical Society I am indebted for a grant in aid of my researches. I want especially to thank Robert D. Cross, Professor of History at Columbia University and editor of this series, for his discerning criticism and extraordinary patience.

Contents

PROLOGUE

ON January 19, 1871, two groups of important Irishmen waited impatiently in the bitter cold of the New York waterfront for the Cunard steamer *Cuba* to appear in the bay. On board were five young Irish revolutionaries who had been released from prison by the British government under the Amnesty Act of the previous year. When the *Cuba* was sighted, cannon boomed and torches flared along the waterfront. Two harbor boats raced each other across the soiled waters in an effort to be the first to send a reception committee aboard. The victorious boat carried Thomas Murphy, the city's Republican boss and Collector of the Port. He bore the greetings of President Grant's administration. The second boat brought out an anxious group of Tammany Hall chieftains. They had raised $25,000 with which to honor the released Fenians and had reserved elegant rooms for them at the Metropolitan Hotel. Murphy was insistent, however, that they accept his invitation to stay at the Astor House. Tempers flared, and the reception threatened to break down into a brawl. The *Cuba* Five thereupon refused to become the property of either party. They remained aboard that night and the next day took up residence amidst the modest comforts of Sweeney's Hotel.

Only two of the *Cuba* Five would long remain in the public eye after the season of welcoming banquets closed. Jeremiah O'Donovan Rossa, whose sufferings at the hands of his jailers had been a matter of parliamentary debate, would within a few years become famous as an Irish exponent of terrorism. In the 1880's he was given to boasting of responsibility for the dynamiters who slipped into English cities with nitroglycerine in their traveling bags. A somewhat demented and very angry Englishwoman shot and wounded him one day in 1885 as he was strolling down Broadway. After a lifetime of revolutionary activity, most of it deplored by fellow nationalists, he died in 1915. For all his ferocity in public life, he was an amiable man and the father of eighteen children. He was buried with a great display of national feeling in Glasnevin Cemetery, Dublin.

Of very different quality was John Devoy. Only twenty-nine when greeted that cold day by Collector Murphy, he was shrewd and hard beyond his years. He had undergone a toughening process in the French Foreign Legion before he took up the assignment of enlisting British Army soldiers of Irish origins for the Irish Revolutionary Brotherhood, the analogue of the Irish-American Fenian Brotherhood from which the generic name Fenian comes. Short, pugnacious, and very intelligent, he would in the years ahead serve as foreign editor of the New York *Herald* and found two newspapers of his own in New York, the *Irish Nation* (1881–85), and the *Gaelic American* (1903–   ). Until his death in 1928, he would be the ideologue, the Lenin, of Irish-American nationalism.

One of the British Army Irishmen whom Devoy brought into the Fenian movement was John Boyle O'Reilly. A lithe and handsome man, with a remarkable capacity for friendship, he arrived in Philadelphia in November, 1869, after a daring escape in an American whaling ship from the British penal colony at Bunbury, Australia. Within a few months after landing, he had established himself in Boston as a lecturer, poet, and staff member of the Boston *Pilot*. Six years later, at the age of thirty-two, he was the editor and co-owner, along with Archbishop John J. Williams of Boston. In the critical years ahead, he would become Boston's favorite Irishman, the poet called upon to write the dedicatory verses for the Plymouth Monument and to serve as mediator between Irish and Puritan Bostonians. He would find the strain of the latter assignment very great and die prematurely in 1890 from an accidental overdose of sleeping pills.

These Fenian exiles would share or rather contest the leadership of the Irish–American community in the 1880's with many others. In Chicago there was Long John Finerty, a Galway man with a reputation as a classicist who, in Irish–American affairs, displayed a most unclassical immoderation. The year in which the *Cuba* Five arrived, he was appointed city editor of the Chicago *Republican*. In 1876 he went out as a war correspondent with General George Crook's expedition against the Sioux and the Northern Cheyennes and wrote dispatches that have won him a substantial place in American frontier history. From 1883 to 1885, he served as a Member of Congress, where he gained a reputation as a comic nationalist. Once upon being asked if anything of interest had taken place that day in the House debate, he answered, "No, nothing but American business today." Annually on August 15 Finerty presided over a United Irish Societies of Chicago picnic at Ogden's Grove, where amidst food and drink the nationalist faith was revitalized. ("Be hivins if Ireland cud be freed by a picnic," said Mr. Dooley, Finley Peter Dunne's stockyard philosopher, "it'd not only be free today but an empire.") In 1882 Finerty founded the Chicago *Citizen*, which he edited until his death in 1908.

Equally immoderate and vastly more influential was Patrick Ford, co-owner and editor of the *Irish World* of New York. Born in Galway in 1837, he was brought to Boston at the age of seven. Like William Lloyd Garrison on whose *Liberator* he learned to be a printer and journalist, Ford was an earnest and highly doctrinaire reformer. Under his editorship the *Irish World* in the 1870's became one of the most remarkable papers in the history of American journalism. Sensational headlines and drawings (tearful Erin crouching in terror over her unstrung harp under the blooded lash of John Bull) anticipated the techniques of yellow journalism, but in substance the paper was very serious indeed. In its pages able and highly individualistic—if sometimes eccentric—correspondents discussed complex matters ranging from the labor theory of value to the teachings of moral theology on land and rents. Ford had been strongly influenced by Boston.

He was moralistic and shrill, given to expressions of righteous violence that were thick with the Old Testament. He oscillated wildly between the two extremes of universal humanitarianism and Irish terrorism. Many thought him a humbug. "He is a totally ignorant, highly unscrupulous, and throughly ill-conditioned fanatic," said John O'Leary, the romantic nationalist whom Yeats mourns in the poem quoted as the epigraph of this book. More than anyone else, Ford brought to the events of the 1870's and 1880's that lofty if querulous idealism which moved the antislavery reformers before the Civil War.

Another Chicagoan was Alexander Sullivan. Born in Canada in 1847, this slender, boyish-looking lawyer possessed a remarkably keen mind, a ruthless will, and a very great determination to get ahead in the world. Early active in Chicago politics, he was appointed clerk of the Board of Public Works in 1873. Three years later he shot and killed a Chicago school principal in a quarrel over school patronage policies, but was acquitted when a jury accepted his plea of self-defense. In the 1880's he became known to the public at large as the leading American Irish supporter of the Republican party and to the Irish revolutionary underworld as the sinister head of the "Triangle," which was presumed to direct the campaign of dynamite terrorism in Britain. In 1889 his power was shattered when he was implicated in the murder of a Chicago physician and long-time antagonist. Old but unsubstantiated charges that he had embezzled Irish nationalist funds and betrayed the dynamiters were then widely publicized. In the history of Chicago he is remembered as an iron-nerved bully and briber of juries. But it should be noted that many good men had confidence in Alexander Sullivan.

In May, 1870, about the time that John Boyle O'Reilly was settling down to his job on the *Pilot*, Michael Davitt was arrested in London on a charge of serving as a Fenian arms agent. He was sentenced to fifteen years, of which, in the 1870's, he would serve a month less than eight. Though he never made his home in the United States, he visited it often in the course of his nationalist career. More than any other Irishman of his generation he touched the hearts of the immigrant peoples of America. They saw him as one of their own. Born in County Mayo in 1846, raised not far from Manchester in a Lancashire factory town, where he worked as a child and lost his right arm in a factory accident, he was of the peasantry and knew the life of the working-class poor. He sensed, with Patrick Ford, that Ireland's poverty was somehow bound up with the suffering of the disinherited everywhere: Mayo, Manchester, and Lowell, Massachusetts, were part of the same pattern of poverty. With courage and imagination, he tried to understand the pattern. The effort had unexpected consequences for him and for Irish nationalism.

All of these gifted men labored under great difficulties. Lacking the securities of wealth, family connections, and social acceptance, they were under constant pressure to justify their leadership. As a consequence all were afflicted with certain temptations: despair and extremism, jealousy and cynicism. In the tangled history of Alexander Sullivan both jealousy and cynicism have parts to play.

While real enough, their leadership was restricted to a narrow range of possibilities. As nationalists they stood, above all, for Irish unity, but inherited from the past was a legacy of divisive hatred and violence. How intractable were the materials of Irish life was apparent in the Orange-Green riots that surged through the streets of New York on July 12, 1870 and 1871. On both occasions, North of Ireland Protestants, bearing the saffron banner of their champion, William of Orange, and chanting "To hell with the Pope," clashed with mobs of Irish Catholics. In 1871 only a murderous volley from the 84th Regiment drove the Catholics off. Like the people they led, the nationalists were prisoners of history. And history had not been kind to the Irish.

What good did emancipation do us? Are we not as naked as we were . . . and eating dry potatoes when we can get them?

A peasant inquiry of a priest,
quoted in GEORGE CORNEWALL LEWIS,
On Local Disturbances in Ireland (London, 1836), p. 109.

The horizon of their thoughts was bounded by the parish in which they lived, or at best by the county, and an Irish nation was a phrase to which no real meaning was attached.

A nationalist's comment on the peasantry,
quoted in CHARLES GAVAN DUFFY, *Four Years of Irish History* (London, 1883), p. 690.

CHAPTER ONE

Nationalist and Peasant

THE turbulent American Irish came from a land long fabled for its troubles. Ireland entered modern history with its ancient Gaelic culture in an advanced stage of decay and its people reeling under the successive blows of an expansive English Protestantism. The Irish surrender at the Siege of Limerick (1691) to the forces of William of Orange led to the collapse of the old Catholic leadership. The O'Donnells, the Lallys, and the rest fled to the courts and armies of Catholic Europe, leaving their people and their lands to the conquerors.

The Ireland which survived was a country divided against itself. In the eastern areas of the northern province of Ulster, Presbyterians of Scottish Lowland origins lived in savage proximity to the Catholics whom their ancestors had been brought over to displace. (It was the descendants of these Ulstermen who flaunted William of Orange's banner before the Catholic Irish of New York in 1871.) Elsewhere, Catholics constituted an overwhelming majority of the population, but their wretched lives were dominated by a small minority of Anglo-Irish members of the Established Church of Ireland, proprietors of the great estates compiled from Catholic lands confiscated in the wars of the sixteenth and seventeenth centuries. Anglo-Irish power was but-

1

tressed by the Penal Laws enacted between 1695 and 1746. Among other things, these oppressive measures denied Catholics the right to hold land on leases of more than thirty-one years, practice the professions, or hold civil or military office. The Catholic hierarchy was banished, and severe limitations were placed on Catholic worship. Although these burdens were progressively lifted in the late eighteenth and early nineteenth centuries, the imbalance in favor of the Anglo-Irish Ascendancy endured. They lived in their big houses like feudal lords, running the affairs of the county, dispensing justice, and collecting rents from the sea of native Irish surrounding them. Relations between the Ascendancy aristocrat and the native Irish peasant were as ambivalent as those between the American slaveowner and the slave.

The Ascendancy presided over a crazy world in which land held the key to life, and competition for it was brutal. The great proprietors rented land to the great tenants—holders in some instances of thousands of acres, who in turn sublet to others, who sublet to lesser men, and so on. At the bottom of the heap were the cottiers, scratching out a living on an acre of land of which they had the use in return for labor. Catholics held land chiefly as tenants at will, subject to eviction should they fail to meet their rents or otherwise give offense. Despite their insecurity of tenure, they too rented off a portion of their holdings. From one point of view, Ireland was a nation of tenant farmers; from another, a nation of petty landlords, competing for land and rents and grinding each other down in the process.

The chief force behind the scramble for land was the rapid expansion of the Irish population beginning in the last half of the eighteenth century. Between 1780 and 1840, the number of Irish increased from approximately 5,000,000 to over 8,000,000. With Irish trade and manufacturing stagnant after 1800, the burden of supporting the expansion fell upon Irish agriculture. Irish farms were divided and subdivided by the tenant farmers to provide holdings for the new generations. "Every patch produces a new family," wrote an observer in 1822; "every member of a family a new patch. . . . Hence a country covered with beggars—a complete pauper warren."

As grain prices fell following the Napoleonic war, necessitating more efficient production, the landlords began to put a stop to the subdivision of their land and to clear out the pauper warrens. By the thousands, the poor were driven off the land. As evictions mounted, the peasantry turned to terrorism to keep their grip on the land. Drawing most of their members from among the cottiers and farmers' sons, whom the movement against subdivision would leave landless, these "Whiteboys" employed cruelty and violence to control the letting of land and the wages of labor.

Whiteboyism was chiefly a war of the poor against the poor. A farmer who employed a laborer from outside the district might be warned by night visitors to discharge him. If he failed to comply, a bit of burning turf might be thrust into the thatch of his cottage or he might be seriously beaten or worse. A peasant who took over a holding from which another was evicted did so in peril of his life. The gentry, or "strong farmers," who offended by keeping grazing land out of tillage might awaken in the morning to discover that during the night terrorists had severed the leg tendons of their cattle. The "squireens" serving as land agents or middlemen, though thoroughly detested, were less vulnerable to attack because of their sturdier houses and their firearms. The great landlords were similarly protected. Moreover, there was in many districts faith in the gentry as the protectors of the poor against the landgrabbing peasant and the grasping squireen.[1]*

Whiteboy violence was invariably motivated by specific local grievances connected with the disposal of land and labor. In the eastern counties of Ulster, where Catholics and Protestants competed for the land, religious differences were an additional factor. But elsewhere, in seeking redress of his grievances, the terrorist was non-sectarian. "The Whitefeet are a most liberal people," testified a priest in 1832, "for they make no distinction between Catholic and Protestant."[2]

* Superior figures refer to Notes at end of text.

It was the potato that sustained this ramshackle society. Nourishing and easily cultivated, it was the staple of the Irish diet and, for the lower orders, virtually the only food consumed. It fostered a dangerous improvidence. Irish boys and girls married young and raised large families in smoky, one-room huts. They were a hospitable people, as every traveler testified. And in spite of the desperate circumstances of their lives, or perhaps because of them, they were not unhappy. They danced and sang, and they fought, with a fierce joy, their faction fights in which feuding kinship groups pummeled each other on festive occasions. But they danced on the edge of a precipice, for they were utterly dependent upon the potato. When it failed and rotted in the ground, as happened repeatedly in the 1830's and then catastrophically in 1845 and 1846, the people suffered starvation. Over a million died in the Great Famine (1845–51) from hunger or famine-induced illness. Another million fled to take up life anew in other lands. The practice of subdividing the land was almost everywhere stopped, and emigration became part of the Irish way of life.

It was in this unpromising soil, salted with tears and rancor, that modern Irish nationalism took root. The first leaders came from the Ascendancy. Jonathan Swift, the great satirist and Dean of St. Parick's Cathedral, Dublin, employed his pen early in the eighteenth century to attack English injustice. Later, when the American revolutionary movement was taking shape, Henry Grattan became the champion of the Ascendancy patriots. Like the American revolutionary leaders, these Protestant Irishmen resented England's reluctance to grant them the rights of Englishmen and out of this resentment forged the material for a new nationalism.

The Irish Parliament in Dublin, from which Catholics were barred, like the American colonial assemblies, was subject to control by the British Parliament at Westminster, and the Irish economy like the American was subordinated to the interests of

English merchants. During the course of the American Revolution a Protestant militia called the Irish Volunteers was organized. Originally inspired by fears of a Catholic uprising in conjunction with a French invasion, the Volunteers soon became a force for constitutional reform. At a convention held at Dungannon, County Tyrone, in February, 1782, the Volunteers—emboldened by American successes—demanded freedom from England's galling trade restrictions and recognition of the Dublin Parliament's independence under the Crown. The Dungannon demands were subsequently accepted by George III's troubled government, and Grattan declared that now "Ireland is a nation."

In the eighteen years that followed, Ireland—or at least its governing classes—prospered. Industry developed, trade flourished, and agricultural prices rose under the influence of expanding wartime markets and protective legislation enacted by the Irish Parliament. Nationalists would later look back upon the period as a golden age.

Nevertheless, the experiment was a failure. The American and French revolutions had aroused exaggerated hopes for reform measures that would admit Catholics to Parliament and wipe out the political corruption that still rendered Irish political life subject to English influence. But these hopes were not to be realized. The Ascendancy feared that its prerogatives would not survive a Catholic restoration, and the strong tide of conservatism set in motion against the French Revolution made London hostile to additional political reform.

Meanwhile, Theobald Wolfe Tone, the son of a Dublin coachmaker, touched by a gay genius and strongly influenced by French radicalism, had in 1791 taken the lead in organizing the Society of United Irishmen to further the cause of reform. When events in 1794–95 made it apparent that reforms were not forthcoming, the United Irishmen went underground and began plotting revolution. Aided by French financial and military support, efforts were made to establish an Irish republic. They failed miserably.

The most dangerous uprising took place in Wexford in 1798, where a desperate Catholic peasantry, goaded by government brutality, took up their pikes. After six bloody weeks they were scattered to the winds. The Wexford Rising was a *Jacquerie*, a revolt of peasants driven by ancestral hatreds and fears, not by concern for the Rights of Man. It was not at all what the United Irishmen had in mind. Under the leadership of the younger Pitt, the British government took advantage of the ensuing demoralization of Ireland to push through the Irish Parliament the Act of Union which, in January 1801, abolished the independent Irish Parliament and merged the Kingdoms of England and Ireland. Thereafter, the Westminster Parliament would legislate for England and Ireland.

The Act of Union reshaped Irish politics. In the following decades the British Parliament became the focus of Irish discontent. And Daniel O'Connell, a new champion of Irish interests, came forward. From an old family of Catholic gentry, whose members had retained their holdings throughout the eighteenth century by using their wits, O'Connell performed the historic task of bringing the native Catholic peoples of Ireland into modern political life.

At the head of the massive Catholic Association he extorted from a Tory government in 1829 the Catholic Relief Act, which at last opened up the Westminster Parliament and all but the highest civil and military offices to Catholics throughout the British Isles. Thereafter, until his death in 1847, O'Connell dominated Irish politics. His admirers called him the Liberator; his enemies, "scum condensed of Irish bog, ruffian, coward, demagogue." But his accomplishments, however great, did not get to the heart of Irish difficulties. Evictions and violence increased in the countryside, while elsewhere—excepting Presbyterian Belfast—trade and manufacturing declined under the pressure of British competition. "What good did emancipation do us? Are we not as naked as we were . . . and eating dry potatoes when we can get them?" a peasant asked of a priest.

In 1840, after more than a decade of disappointing effort to win London's support for the amelioration of Irish grievances, O'Connell founded the National Repeal Association for the purpose of repealing the Act of Union and restoring an Irish parliament. Two years later three young nationalists, Thomas Davis, Charles Gavan Duffy, and John Blake Dillon, gave the Repeal movement an enormous boost by founding the Dublin *Nation*, the most brilliant and influential paper in nationalist history. Young Ireland, as the *Nation*'s editors and followers came to be called, were destined to quarrel with O'Connell. The issues dividing them, magnified in retrospect, would divide later generations of nationalists in Ireland and America.

The Repeal agitation reached its climax in 1843, when the Repeal Association summoned the people by the tens of thousands at various historic sites to hear the Liberator call for the restoration of an Irish parliament in language more militant and threatening than he perhaps intended. Now sixty-eight, O'Connell was close to the end of a life devoted to making moral persuasion a substitute for violence. His words on these occasions nevertheless excited his followers and alarmed the government. More troops were moved into Ireland, and the final "monster meeting" scheduled for Clontarf, where eight hundred years before the Irish had driven the Danes into the sea, was banned by the authorities in Dublin Castle. To the disgust of many, O'Connell called off the meeting, and thereafter the steam went out of the movement.

The quarrel between O'Connell and Young Ireland blossomed in the following years. It came about partly because of circumstances. O'Connell was old and jealous of his authority; they were young and impatient. They were, for the most part, middle-class Protestants, excessively earnest and moralistic. He had the gift of gab, carried his Catholicism easily, and affronted them by his casuistry.

But the matter went deeper than personalities. O'Connell was a realist who had taken up Repeal, not because of any doctrinaire belief in nationality, but because experience had convinced him that within the Union Ireland could not expect to get a fair shake. To Young Ireland, however, the question was not simply one of political or social justice, but was concerned with the claims of a proud nation to its own identity.

> Though Englishmen were to give us the best tenure on earth, though they were to equalize Presbyterian, Catholic, and Episcopalian, though they were to give us the completest representation in their parliament . . . we would still tell them . . . that we spurned the offer if the conditions were that Ireland remain a Province.[3]

O'Connell's mind was shaped in the eighteenth century. However much he appeared a demagogue, he was a man of restraint and moderation. He shared with his generation a repugnance for the French Revolution. For Tone and the United Irishmen—the overreachers—he had contempt. The Young Irelanders, on the other hand, had been among the first to resurrect the reputation of Tone. They liked his courage and daring; his life was a romance.

The Young Irelanders were romantics, indebted to the English and Continental romantics, to Carlyle and other critics of the liberal-industrialized societies emerging in Western Europe. They had serious reservations about the modern world into which O'Connell was dragging Ireland. They convicted it of Utilitarianism, by which they meant a sordid materialism, indifferent to beauty and idealism. "To make our people politically free but bond slaves to some debasing social system like that which crowds the mines and factories of England with squalid victims, we would not strike a blow," declared the *Nation*. But in Ireland where the "debasing currents of European civilization only visit at high tide, there is still a place for a great experiment for humanity."[4]

Young Ireland's concerns went beyond politics. The young men were moral reformers who would raise up a new nation that would be a city upon a hill and a judgment upon English civilization. Their ideal was an inclusive nationalism to which Catholic and Protestant, peasant and landlord, Gael and Anglo-Irish, could give their loyalty. They looked to history for the materials that would provide the national mind with noble thoughts and rid it of the religious, regional, and class hatreds that sickened it. Davis turned his hand to historical verse and ballads. Duffy inaugurated the Library of Ireland, a series of historical and biographical studies, some of which would go through many editions, providing Irish and Irish-American apologists with propaganda for generations to come.

The break with the O'Connellites came in 1846, when the Repeal Association adopted a resolution condemning any recourse to violence to attain its ends. Because their orthodox nationalism affirmed the ultimate right of revolution, the young men withdrew from the Association. Not that in 1846 they were plotting revolution. They still stood for Repeal, and their hopes were pinned on the slow processes of education and agitation. They hoped especially to win over the Ascendancy aristocrats, descendants of the men who had joined the Irish Volunteers over half a century earlier.

Young Ireland had taken the lead in 1845 of founding the Eighty-Two Club in the anticipation that by evoking the memory of Grattan they could win over the gentry. Two years later, with the same hopes in mind, they founded the Irish Confederation. Neither effort amounted to much more than speeches and gaudy uniforms. Significantly, the Irish Confederation received its greatest support outside of Ireland, in the English and Scottish industrial cities to which the despairing emigrants had fled. In Manchester and across the Irwell in Salford, the very heartland of the dark satanic mill country which Davis had deplored, membership in the Confederate clubs numbered 500.[5]

Young Ireland was caught in a dilemma. The landed gentry, Grattan's Protestant nation, after the bloody Rising of 1798 and Catholic Emancipation, were less disposed than ever to trust the Catholic nation. The connection with Britain had become sanctified in their minds as the protector of their property and their Protestantism. Short of a fundamental change in their attitudes, only a revolution could realize Repeal. But revolution meant breaking with the gentlemen of education and polish whose mansions graced the Irish countryside. Did they not—at least the responsible among them—provide the materials for Young Ireland's idealized Ireland that stood in contrast to England's graceless industrialism? They were at any rate men of manners and status for whom these middle-class nationalists felt an instinctive deference.

To break with the gentry meant falling back upon the peasantry, upon the savage Wexford men and the secret terrorists, upon that deranged Gaelic Ireland to whom the young nationalists addressed their moral essays. The difficulties involved in such a choice are hard for us to appreciate. It is as though a Montgomery shopkeeper today were asked to throw in his lot with the Negro sharecropper of the Alabama backwoods. The Young Irelanders neither knew nor trusted the peasantry.[6]

It was the Great Famine that forced the choice upon them. In 1847, when three of the eight million Irish were receiving famine relief and the dead and dying were everywhere, the issue was raised by the deaf and deformed son of a County Queens gentleman. In a remarkable series of letters to the *Nation*, James Fintan Lalor argued that only by embracing the peasant's cause of land reform could Young Ireland break out of its dilemma. Lalor's ideas resembled in a striking way those advanced in the 1880's by Patrick Ford, Michael Davitt, and Henry George, the greatest of the land reformers. Not that Lalor was a primary influence upon them, as nationalist historians would have it; rather, all were shocked by the Industrial Revolution's impact upon the traditional agrarian order and all looked for solutions in the same grab bag of ideas inherited from eighteenth-century natural rights thought. Lalor's genius, and George's, was to find there materials meaningful to their times.

Lalor argued that in a body politic formed freely by man ultimate political sovereignty and ownership of land lay with the whole people—the nation. Because the Irish nation had never given its assent to English claims of sovereignty and Anglo-Irish claims of land ownership, these claims were without moral basis. Now with the Great Hunger dissolving society, with the social compact broken, the time was ripe for the Irish nation to recover its own.

In this analysis the political and social revolutions merged and were theoretically of equal importance. But in the context of Irish life the social revolution held primacy. A purely political movement for repeal of the Union was bound to fail because it would be exclusively a middle-class enterprise. Neither the gentry nor the peasantry would support it. The land-hungry peasant, however, would fight for a social upheaval that would give him what he wanted. There was, said Lalor, a "wolf dog" in every Irish cabin. "For repeal . . . he will never bite but only bay." But for possession of a piece of land he would bite and bite savagely. The Young Irelanders, therefore, should link their political movement to the peasant's land hunger, like a "railway carriage to the engine."[7]

Lalor's argument made a strong impression on the *Nation's* staff, but after debate the majority rejected it. It would, they believed, cut whatever ties remained with the aristocracy and displace a national movement motivated by chivalry by a class war dominated by greed. It would touch off a *Jacquerie,* like the Wexford Rising in 1798. But for John Mitchel, a powerful writer of northern Presbyterian origins, and a handful of others Lalor's general argument made sense. It was better to encourage the people to risk, if necessary, a violent revolution than to accept death by starvation.

Mitchel broke with the majority, and in the *United Irishman,* which he founded in February, 1848, he encouraged the peasantry to refuse payment of rents and rates (taxes). But Mitchel did not know the peasantry, and they did not know him. In April he was attacked by a mob at Limerick. In the following month the government imprisoned him under a recently passed act that made treasonable speech a common felony. He was sentenced to fourteen years and dispatched to the prison colony at Bermuda.

Before the summer of 1848 was over, events forced the Young Ireland majority to follow Mitchel into revolution. The success of the Parisians in overthrowing the French monarchy in February, 1848, without serious bloodshed aroused hopes in Young Ireland for a similar success. But as they stumbled forward in their planning, the government moved in troops. In July it laid down what amounted to an ultimatum by suspending the writ of habeas corpus. The Young Irelanders were forced to fight or face arrest. They were honorable men, and they made the decision to fight.

But they had nothing to fight with: no arms, no men. They hoped the shimmering ideal of freedom would rally the people. "From earliest childhood to that hour," wrote Michael Doheny later of his feelings as he left to join the rising, "I never met an Irishman whose hope it was not to deliver the country forever from England's thrall."[8]

The rebels first tried to arouse the townspeople of Kilkenny and Tipperary; that failing, they then fell back upon the peasantry. But the rebels had nothing to offer. Some proposed promising the people land in return for support, but this was rejected by the scrupulous Smith O'Brien, a Protestant landed aristocrat who had committed his sacred honor to the Young Ireland cause. It all ended with token bloodletting in a cabbage garden in Ballingarry, County Tipperary, where the Young Irelanders proved themselves gentlemen, if not competent revolutionaries. After escaping to a ship bound for America, Doheny bitterly blessed the "wildest waves that bear me from a land of slaves."

These events pointed up the difficulties nationalists faced in trying to overthrow so resolute and confident a people as the British with so divided a people as the Irish. The richest and most powerful Irish—the Anglo-Irish—were committed to the British connection. The middle classes were too few in number and too

unsure of themselves to go it alone. Peasant support was imperative and yet, for a number of reasons, hard to command.

The Young Irelander, quoted in this chapter's epigraph, who
asserted that the peasant had no conception of an Irish nation
was no doubt wrong. But it is true that peasant and nationalist
conceived of Ireland in different ways. Young Ireland was a
product of English culture; its values were not those of the Gael.
The Young Irelander wanted the peasant to act in the name of an
abstraction called the Irish nation, but his loyalties inhered in
more concrete relationships—those of the family, the parish, the
village, and Whiteboy society. The peasant followed leaders, not
principles, and for the most part, he looked to the priest or the
landlord or both for leadership. O'Connell's mass movement in
behalf of Catholic emancipation, for example, rested on the
shoulders of the parish priests. But their support was not given to
Young Ireland whose criticism of sectarianism had rendered them
suspect of being indifferent to religion or even atheistic in the
style of continental nationalism.

Moreover, no view of Irish life that did not give primacy to
peasant concerns, especially that of the land question, could long
hold the peasantry. Not that Lalor's formula held the answer.
Mitchel in 1848 and Lalor himself in 1849 tried to arouse the
people on the basis of the land question and both failed disastrously. The structure of rural life in these years was all but
closed to such efforts. With both priests and landlords opposed,
the nationalist could not readily build up grass roots support.

But the tide of events was moving in the direction of nationalism. The Great Famine swept away the old Handy Andy Ireland
and accelerated the process of anglicization. Before the famine
perhaps half the population was Gaelic-speaking, and illiteracy in
English was high. As the Gaeltacht shrunk and illiteracy in English declined, nationalist propaganda was given opportunities
not available earlier. Though the Irish educational system was designed to make "happy English boys," it brought Irish youth into
contact with those European ideas upon which nationalism fed.

The breakup of so many of the old feudal holdings, encouraged by the Encumbered Estates Act of 1849, dissolved the traditional ties that had held peasant and landlord together. Not being of the "quality," the new landlords could not command the respect and awe of their predecessors. Faction fighting and the old regional animosities declined after the Famine, bringing the peasant people into closer accord.

Within the nationalist movement, two traditions were established by the events of the 1840's and 1850's: the parliamentary and the revolutionary. The former stemmed from O'Connell. It believed in political action within the British constitutional system. It recalled O'Connell's great success in winning Catholic Emancipation from the British Parliament, and it looked forward to the establishment of a unified parliamentary party that would control enough votes in the House of Commons to make that body receptive to Irish demands.

Following the Famine, an effort along these lines was made to save the tenant farmer from ruin. An independent Irish party was organized, pledged to tenant reforms and to the defense of Catholic interests. It prospered for a time and then ran onto the rocks. Nationalists placed the blame upon two ambitious Catholics, John Sadleir and William Keogh, who sold out the party for government positions, and upon Paul Cullen, Catholic Archbishop of Dublin, who withdrew his support because he feared the movement was infected with the atheistic nationalism of the Continent. The basic cause, however, was due to the party's failure to build up local organizations that could rival the influence of priest and landlord.[9]

For those who adhered to the revolutionary tradition the independent party's failure was proof that parliamentary action was a fraud and Parliament itself a place where Irishmen were certain to suffer corruption. That throughout most of the 1840's the Young Irelanders no less than O'Connell stood for parliamentary action and moral persuasion was all but forgotten. It was Young Ireland's last-ditch recourse to physical force that was most vividly remembered. They were regarded as pure revolutionaries who preferred to risk death rather than dishonor their principles by any compromise with the "bloody British bull." John Mitchel became the living symbol of this "pure nationalism." It asserted that English rule was without moral justification, that Irishmen who cooperated with it by taking seats in Parliament were acting immorally, and that the only rightful course was to prepare for revolution. O'Connell's moral persuasion was disparaged, and the God of battles was invoked.

The Fenian movement, which in the 1860's caught up Devoy, Davitt, O'Reilly, and others in its turmoil, was of this persuasion. The Fenian Rising in 1867 was only slightly less ludicrous than Young Ireland's in 1848. But failure did not diminish the revolutionary's appeal for the young and idealistic. Each generation added new names to an old martyrology.

Neither of these traditions alone would know triumph in the nineteenth century. Not until the adherents of both came together in a grand alliance in the 1880's would great success be won. In that success the American Irish, descendants of those who fled the Great Famine, would play a critical part.

Out of Ireland have we come.
Great hatred, little room,
Maimed us at the start.
I carry from my mother's womb
A fanatic heart.
                    WILLIAM BUTLER YEATS

I might as well have been born in Boston. . . . I brought nothing
with me from Ireland . . . nothing tangible to make me what
I am.

                                        PATRICK FORD

CHAPTER TWO

The Fanatic Heart

O VER three million Irish came to the United States in the years between the onset of the Famine in 1846 and the death of Parnell in 1891. The immigrant tide ebbed and flowed according to the push and pull of conditions in Great Britain and the United States. It was at flood in 1851, when more than 221,000 entered and lowest in the depression year of 1877, when fewer than 15,000 came over. The provinces of Munster and Connacht, in the South and West, suffered the greatest losses, but Ulster in the North and the rich land of Leinster were stripped as well. The sons and daughters of Ireland's laborers and small farmers got out; pushed off the land to make way for cattle, they saw that Ireland offered them little and America a great deal. "The wheat pulled up," an Irishman lamented in the dark year of 1847, "and the tares left." However true for the year 1847, this was too melodramatic a judgment to describe a process that soon became a fixed institution in Irish life: as children came of age the rural family made a decision as to who should go and who should stay. For those designated to leave, the choice was largely either the cities of the United States or those of Great Britain. Before the Famine, Britain was favored; afterward, until the end of the nineteenth century, the great majority chose the United States.

The Famine immigrants landed in the United States like tired migratory birds. Prisoners of poverty, they were confined to the cities in which they landed or to those of the interior, on rivers, canals, and railways, where work was available. They had not been prepared by the potato culture of Ireland for the hard ways of the frontier; nor had it provided them with the capital and skills with which to take over the land the Yankees left behind.

Those who emigrated after the first great wave of Famine victims adhered for the most part to the pattern of urban settlement already laid down. Many earnest efforts would be made to reshape the pattern so as to establish communities of Irish in the new farmlands of the West, but without substantial success. The Irish preferred the bright lights of the city and needed the employment it afforded.

The United States Census for 1890, when the number of Irish-born was at an all-time high of 1,872,000, recorded that only a little more than 2 per cent of them were engaged in agriculture. Most were bunched in the great cities: Boston, New York, Philadelphia, Chicago, St. Louis, and San Francisco. In New York and Brooklyn together there were more persons of Irish birth or origin than there were in Dublin. In Boston, persons of Irish origin constituted a majority. In the nation as a whole there were nearly 5,000,000 persons of Irish birth or origin, some 200,000 more than the population of Ireland and approximately one-twelfth of the total number of Americans.

Everywhere in the United States the Irish provided a pool of cheap, unskilled labor. In the factories of Lowell, Massachusetts, and Troy, New York, in the mines of Scranton, Pennsylvania, and Leadville, Colorado, and amidst the construction gangs and servant force of American cities, they found places that offered some realization of the promise of American life. In many ways the New World was as full of hardships and uncertainties as the Old. Rents were high, and during bad times wages barely covered subsistence. The tenements of Boston's Fort Hill, New York's Five Points, and Chicago's Bridgeport were as unhealthy as the wretched huts of Ireland's West and Southwest. While in the last quarter of the century, the sons and grandsons of the first immigrants were making their way into the middle classes, the recent arrival and his family were perpetuating the reality that a great portion of America's poor were of Irish origins.

It is easy to sentimentalize the immigrant experience. They were a tough-minded people, and emigration was soon accepted as part of the pattern of life, which in any event no one expected to be easy. Nevertheless, even for the stoic the experience was not without its disillusionments. The Irish image of the United States was that of a greater and more benevolent Ireland, an image sustained by the family ties that stretched across the Atlantic and by the flow of remittance money that helped pay rents as well as finance the emigration of still other members of the family.

But the reality was otherwise. Like the immigrants from continental Europe, the Irish had a painful adjustment to make in America. Their possession of the English language gave them advantages denied other immigrants, but at the same time it brought them more directly and abrasively into contact with American culture. Out of the contact would emerge that fierce nationalism which would in the 1880's send Irish-American dynamiters, land reformers, and political agitators moving stormily across the Atlantic in the hope of changing the face and mind of Ireland.

The Irish brought few possessions with them when they embarked for America. They had little in the way of the world's goods and not much in the way of skills. They brought with them an intense Catholicism that had been shaped, perhaps deranged, by the pressures of Ascendancy Protestantism. And they brought memories of the Great Famine.

That terrible tragedy filled the immigrant ships with bitterness. The dispersed Irish felt deep in their hearts that the English government had deliberately contrived to starve them out. In Jim Tully's *Shanty Irish* (1928), we have the folk story told by old Hughie Tully in all its morbid detail: peasants ejected by the thousands, set adrift upon the roads to eat nettles and wild mus-

tard weed, dogs and dead horses; the coffins whose bottoms were hinged to provide for more than one burial and yet preserve the decencies; the departing peasants crammed on emigrant ships that were themselves like coffins, seeing with sickened eyes ships loaded with Irish grain outward bound to Liverpool; and then more dying and dead. But this was not the only worm eating at the Irish heart. There was another: the fury of the Irish with themselves for letting it happen. "They died like whipped curs a-whinnin' under the lash—whimpering from the ditches and the bogs. Holy Mary—Mither of God—pray for us starvin' sinners now an' at the hour of our horrible death—Amen."

Perhaps the Irish who had remained at home did not feel so keenly this aspect of the Great Famine, but for those living among Americans—the people of get-up-and-go to whom poverty was sinful—there was no escaping a sense of humiliation in reflecting on so much suffering so passively endured.

As this second point suggests, Irish-American nationalism was something more than an Irish export. It sprang also from the experience of life in the United States. First of all, the Irish, like all immigrants, were afflicted with loneliness. To quiet its pangs, the immigrants came together in social clubs and gathering places of many kinds: firefighting brigades, literary clubs, militia companies, corner saloons. All afforded Irishmen the comforts of fraternity, and some of them opportunities, not available in parochial Ireland, to intermingle with Irishmen from all parts of their native land. In this way loneliness encouraged a sense of nationality. Not all clubs, of course, had this character. The Charitable Irish Society in Boston and the Friendly Sons of St. Patrick in New York, first founded in the eighteenth century, throughout most of the nineteenth reflected wealth, status, and exclusiveness. Many early militia companies were recruited solely from workers of particular trades, and later in the nineteenth century clubs came into existence in which membership was based upon the immigrant's Irish county of origin.

But on the whole loneliness stimulated nationalism, not particularism. An eloquent expression of the workings of loneliness is provided us by an immigrant bricklayer, Batt O'Connor, who would later return to Ireland to participate in the Irish Revolution of 1916. After his arrival in the United States in 1893, O'Connor was afflicted with melancholia: "I would try to recall the smell of the turf, and I would think of the streams in which I went fishing, and the place where I found a bird's nest. . . ." Ballybeyond could not easily be recaptured by O'Connor, nor by his fellows, but longing for it brought them together and gave them a new awareness of their love for Ireland. For O'Connor, a St. Patrick's Day parade in Providence, Rhode Island, was a kind of epiphany, in which much was revealed to him. "I walked in that procession and in the emotion I felt, walking as one of that vast crowd of Irish emigrants celebrating our national festival, I awoke to the full consciousness of my love for my country."[1]

Immigrant nationalism thus had as one of its sources the all too human melancholia and sense of loss suffered by those who have irrevocably broken with the past that nurtured them. For most, it would probably pass, but for some the ache would be permanent; they would always be aliens in their new land. The anti-English immigrant agitator, wrote an English commentator of perception, was not as the British liked to think a swindler and demagogue, but "that much more unreasonable animal, a dreamer."[2] Within the Irish neighborhoods of the great American cities, older allegiance, carried over from Ireland, found expression in the Kerry Patches, Donegal Squares, and Corkmen's Hollows, which were to be found in virtually all cities. Nevertheless, what counted most was the newly realized sense of all being one because all were Irish. Life in America, said Patrick Ford, lifted the Irishman out of the "littleness of countyism into the broad feeling of nationalism."[3]

But the immigrant nationalist was something more than a dreamer, and he was driven by more than nostalgia for the Old Country. Indeed, it was the ruling passion for many second- and third-generation Irishmen who knew only America. One of the most dedicated nationalists in the period covered in this book was William Mackey Lomasney. He was born in Cincinnati in 1841 of Irish parents who had emigrated from County Cork. He was blown to bits in 1884 while attempting to dynamite London Bridge. Equally committed was Captain John McCafferty. Born in Sandusky, Ohio, in 1838, he had served during the Civil War with Morgan's Confederate guerrillas. He was reputed in later years to be the chief of the Invincibles who assassinated Lord Frederick Cavendish in Dublin's Phoenix Park in 1882. In both of these men there was no doubt something of the adventurer, but there was also a deep and driving bitterness.

Some light on the American sources of the agony felt by men like McCafferty and Lomasney is revealed in the testimony of Patrick Ford. Speaking to an English reporter at the height of the land agitation, for whose successes Ford could claim considerable credit, he admitted that as a youth he had known nothing of Ireland. "I might as well have been born in Boston. . . . I brought nothing with me from Ireland . . . nothing tangible to make me what I am." It was Boston, he insisted, which had shaped his life. At the height of the Know Nothing movement, when an anti-Irish, anti-Catholic wave of feeling swept the nation in the early 1850's, young Ford walked the streets of Boston in search of work and everywhere encountered notices which read: NO IRISH NEED APPLY.

> I went searching in this way for some months . . . finding constantly that the fact that I was Irish and a Catholic was against me. I was not yet awake about Ireland, but I began to think early, to read whatever I could lay my hands on . . . and to think over what I had read.

He finally came to the conclusion that he was the victim of the "conditions of poverty and enslavement" which gripped the land of his birth and to the solemn decision that "it was necessary for everyone of Irish blood to do all in his power to change that state of things."[4]

American hostility against the Irish has a long history, but only with the advent of mass immigration in the 1840's and 1850's did contempt and fear on the part of native Americans and resentment and fear on the Irish side become almost everywhere characteristic of their relations. It was in these tense and unhappy years that the Irish-American community was shaped. The Protestant Irish hastily disassociated themselves from the impoverished Catholics, and some were active in the Know Nothing camp. And in the early years non-Irish Catholics, anxious to preserve the Anglo-American character of the pre-1830 Church, shared some of the nativists' animosities. But the Church like the nation was soon overwhelmed by the immigrant wave and the popular identification, which endures to this day, of Irish with Catholic was established. Thus the battle lines were drawn: Irish Catholic against Anglo-American Protestant. It was not unusual, then, for Patrick Ford to see nativism as primarily an extension of English hatred for the Irish and not unreasonable for him to conclude that the solution to the immigrant's difficulties lay in Ireland.

The springs of Irish-American nationalism, we may conclude, are to be found in the realities of loneliness and alienation, and of poverty and prejudice. For its formal content this peculiar nationalism owed much to the thought and traditions of Tone, O'Connell, and Young Ireland, but it was from life in America that it derived its most distinctive attitudes: a pervasive sense of inferiority, intense longing for acceptance and respectability, and an acute sensitivity to criticism.

It is not easy to determine how far this spirit of resentment cut into the Irish and to what extent it colored their lives. For the women, busy with home and children, it was very likely not a matter of great moment. They were for the most part realists, indifferent to the romantic resentments of their sons and husbands. The Irish working classes had the trade-union movement through which to express their discontent, but in the decade and a half following the Depression of 1873 this movement was profoundly influenced by nationalism.

Always and everywhere the anxieties of nationalism were most characteristic of the ambitious, whose energies had earned them not only the humiliations of the kind described by Ford, but also some degree of economic and social progress. In nationalism they found a rationalization of their pains and in nationalist organizations opportunities for leadership and prestige. It is thus no accident that the second generation were fiercely active in the cause. They wanted to be respected as Americans and this, as the following speech of Michael Davitt suggests, gave immigrant nationalism its dynamic thrust:

> You want to be honored among the elements that constitute this nation. . . . You want to be regarded with the respect due you; that you may thus be looked on, aid us in Ireland to remove the stain of degradation from your birth . . . and [you] will get the respect you deserve.[5]

Humiliation, resentment, and bitterness hardly provide a healthy basis for social action. And admittedly throughout the course of Irish-American nationalism there runs a sustained whine to which on occasion even a man so free of self-pity as John Boyle O'Reilly would contribute. But this offensiveness was offset to some extent by a generosity of spirit that derived from the immigrant's conviction that he was acting in the name of certain values common to all Americans and worthy of all men. He demanded respect for himself but only as a member of the greater American community. He was asking Americans to live up to their highest ideals. This generosity of spirit and sense of human solidarity informed, though it did not determine, all aspects of immigrant nationalism in the early 1880's. Later, when failures multiplied and disillusionment deepened, resentment would smother generosity and the whining would grow louder.

The formation of an Irish-American community at odds with the larger American community had profound consequences.

Thereafter, most American Irish would find it difficult to live their lives solely as individuals, without reference to the Irish-American community. Individuals would, of course, continue to make their way according to pluck and luck, but at some stage of their career they would find themselves tagged as Irish and judged according to the prevailing prejudices. Then, too, they would be made to feel the pull of the Irish-American community and the demands it made for their loyalites. Those demands placed a heavy burden upon the spirit.

In the early years of the nineteenth century, Irishmen like the Dublin-born Mathew Carey were free of this burden. Carey had a brilliant American, not Irish-American, career as a printer, bookseller, and publisher. As a pamphleteer, he addressed himself to the major questions of the day. He did not live in a ghetto. In his most famous work, *The Olive Branch,* written to soften the animosities between Federalist and Jeffersonian, he could boast "I am an Irishman. . . . I glory, I take pride in the name of an Irishman,"[6] and still make an important contribution to national unity. He was active in societies to aid the immigrant poor; and in 1819 he published an important work of Irish apologetics, *Vindiciae Hibernicae, or Ireland Vindicated,* which was designed to convince the British people—then considering a Catholic emancipation bill—that the old charge of Irish savagery at the outset of the 1641 rebellion was without foundation. In the closing years of his life anti-Irish feeling was mounting. Widespread criticism of Irish gang violence on railroad and public works projects elicited from Carey a defense of the immigrant that would have many imitators. In a series of public letters, he declared that immigrant valor in the American Revolution, generosity and family feeling evidenced by the remittances of money to those left behind in Ireland, and heroic labor in building canals and other structures basic to American material growth gave the immigrant a high claim upon the United States. Carey was able to defend the lowly Irish without being identified in the public mind as one of them.

Later apologists would add to his arguments, but few could

speak with his confidence and authority. His death in 1839, marked by nation-wide tributes of respect, all but brought an end to this first period of Irish-Catholic life in the United States. His successors, the Forty-Eighters who came after the abortive Rising of 1848, found a nation sharply divided between Irish and American. Drawn by their loyalties to the former and their liberal sympathies to the latter, they were never able to play Carey's creative role.

The two ablest of them, Thomas D'Arcy McGee and John Mitchel, found the tensions too great. McGee had begun hopefully in 1848 by establishing in New York a new *Nation* that in its brief lifetime was militantly liberal and critical of Catholic support for those European monarchies then crushing nationalist revolts. Very quickly he was attacked by the formidable John Hughes, New York's Catholic Archbishop, who accused him of being a bad Catholic and a bad Irishman. At the same time McGee could find little comfort in the camp of American liberals, then seething with anti-Irish feeling. Caught in this way and concerned about the demoralizing effect American life had upon his countrymen, McGee abandoned liberalism. His second paper, the *American Celt*, soon was dedicated to defending the Faith and the traditional values of conservative Catholic Europe. Restless and ill at ease in America, he went in 1857 to Montreal, Canada, where he found opportunities for leadership denied him in the United States. In the 1860's he played a distinguished part in founding the Canadian Confederation from which modern Canada has sprung. He had by this time infuriated Irish nationalists, who held that his Canadian career constituted a betrayal of Ireland, and in 1868 he was assassinated by a Fenian on an Ottawa street.

John Mitchel had little love for McGee, but he too found Irish life intolerable in the teeming industrial cities of the North. He too brought out a newspaper, the *Citizen*, and encountered the Archbishop's enmity. And he too fled, going in the spring of 1855, after a little more than a year's stay in New York, to East Tennessee. There he first tried farming, and then in 1857 established in

Knoxville his second newspaper, the *Southern Citizen.* Mitchel's instincts had perhaps never been liberal, but his experiences with Northern liberalism, which he judged to be nothing more than a variety of English utilitarianism, elicited from him, as from McGee, a surprising and most thoroughgoing conservatism. The *Southern Citizen* denounced abolitionism and defended slavery. After two years, however, he gave up the paper and sailed for Paris.

Thereafter, his life was a lonely odyssey. Searching for something, he moved back and forth across the Atlantic. Two of his sons joined the Confederacy when war broke out, and in 1862 he left Paris for the Confederate capital at Richmond, where during the course of the war he edited two newspapers. After a brief imprisonment in Fortress Monroe, along with other Confederate leaders, he once again took up residence in Paris. In 1865–66 he served without much enthusiasm, as financial agent of the Fenian Brotherhood, then plotting revolution in Ireland. From 1867 to 1872, he published the *Irish Citizen* in New York, infuriating the Fenians by his disdain for their grandiloquent claims. In 1875 he went back to Ireland to die. As a final act of defiance, he stood for and was elected to the British Parliament as a Member from Tipperary. ". . . I take it that the chief fact about my past life which recommended me to the people of Tipperary was that I had made no peace with England."[7] Mitchel wrote one magnificent book, *The Jail Journal,* but he never really found himself in America. He lived the life of the intransigent exile.

With the Irish-American community a reality after the Civil War, young Irishmen would seek success through leadership in the community's affairs. Outstanding Irishmen in the 1880's, whether businessmen like the somewhat shifty William Onahan of Chicago or politicians like the able Patrick Collins of Boston, were very often dependent upon their ability to exploit the sentiments of Irish-America. They had more room in which to maneuver than had Mitchel and McGee, but much less than Mathew Carey.

In 1856 a federal court warned members of an Irish revolutionary society, euphemistically named the Irish Emigrant Aid Society of Cincinnati, that there "can be no such thing as a divided
allegiance." Rarely, however, did the loyalty issue posed by Irish-
American nationalism come before the courts. The federal structure of American government and the traditional diversity of
American group life fostered a multiplicity of loyalties. The
formula of the Cincinnati court was far too simple to do justice to
the realities. Short of treason, group action in support of European nationalist movements has been tolerated and at times even
encouraged by the American government. Nevertheless, the
charge that such activities were somehow un-American has been
raised repeatedly in American history. Perhaps the single most
important theme in Irish-American literature is that devoted to
justifying immigrant loyalty to Ireland and reconciling it with
their loyalty to the United States. The immigrant's isolation from
the greater American community only intensified his concern.
The task of his leaders was to so interpret his experience that the
tensions created by this ambivalence might be creatively re-
solved.

It was a task that most American ethnic groups would sooner
or later find it necessary to undertake. "The meaningful question,"
as Oscar Handlin has stated, "is not whether loyalties are divided,
but whether they can be justified in terms acceptable to all Americans."[8]

In the labor of justification the Irish had certain unique advantages. Both the American patriot and the Irish-American patriot
were products of English culture; both spoke the same language
and read the same literature. As nationalists, both were engaged
in rejecting English claims to moral and political superiority.
Nineteenth-century Irish nationalism, especially as expressed by
Daniel O'Connell and Charles Stewart Parnell, was preoccupied
with constitutional questions much like those which obsessed
Americans. Both nations had a tradition of hostility to England.
Of all the Catholic peoples of Western Europe, the Irish alone

were without a stake in perpetuating the anti-democratic governments and aristocratic societies of the past. In Wolfe Tone and
other United Irishmen they had national heroes identified with
the liberal revolutionary hopes of the late eighteenth century.

Of great importance in the work of justification was the series
of lectures given by Thomas D'Arcy McGee to packed houses in
cities throughout the East in the period 1850–55. The first lecture,
delivered in 1850–51 and subsequently published as the *History
of the Irish Settlers in North America* (1851), demonstrated,
through a catalogue-like account of Irishmen prominent in early
American history, that the Irish thread was an integral part of the
American fabric. Like Carey's earlier work, *Ireland Vindicated,*
the *Irish Settlers* was thrown together in a hurry and made no
pretension to be either history or literature. It was pure apologia
and very popular.[9]

The second series of lectures were given in the winter of 1853–
54, after McGee had become disillusioned by his American experience. Published in 1855 as *The Catholic History of North America,* these sketched United States history against the broad back-
drop of Catholic Europe and Catholic missionary efforts in New
France and New Spain.

Along with all this, a supplement to the work met squarely
American criticism of the Catholic peasantry daily passing
through American ports—Irishmen so very different from the
Protestant gentlemen who paraded through the *Irish Settlers.*
McGee fell back upon the sensible argument Carey had sketched
out nearly twenty years earlier. Without Irish labor, America's
spectacular material growth would not have been possible. As for
the Irish, they could be confident that someday they would share
in the leadership of the nation they were building.

The realism of this supplement to the *Catholic History* was
less popular than the main work and far less popular than the re-
cital of Irish glories chronicled in the *Irish Settlers,* which ran
through many editions. The latter work was freely plundered by
later apologists. William R. Grace, founder of the Grace Lines

and the first Irish-born Catholic Mayor of New York City, and Honest John Kelly, founder of Tammany Hall's Irish dynasty, were among the many who in the decades following the Civil War freely embellished McGee's histories.

According to the bracing propaganda of these years, an Irishman figured critically in every turning point in American history. The New World was discovered by St. Brendan, the Navigator, and Columbus was rowed ashore at Watling Island by an Irishman. This latter information demonstrated, according to the Boston *Pilot,* "that the Irish is no bastard or corrupt stock, but one of the seminal races of the earth. . . ."[10] As befitted such a people, its soldiers were virtually responsible for winning the American Revolution against the opposition of vicious English and German Protestants; and its blood ran through the veins of innumerable famous Americans, including those of that thumping nativist and inventor of the telegraph, Samuel Finley Breese Morse.

The Irish-American apologist rarely concerned himself with the realities of the Irish-Catholic situation: the poverty and slums, the street gangs and saloons, the priest's influence and the politician's chicanery, the modest aspirations hard-working mothers held for their sons. The apologists preferred to speak of Irish glories. Because of its manifest and sometimes comic distortions and because it put aside problems that were matters of real concern, this propaganda was hardly influential outside the Irish-American community. Its importance lies in the power it had to give the immigrant and his sons a dramatic sense of participation in the American epic. It nourished egos suffering from a sense of humiliation. It assured the Irish poor that they had a stake in the nation's future. To those who branded them aliens, they could answer: "This is our country. We bought it dearly. We like it well, and we intend to stay."

McGee's system of apologetics established the antiquity of Irish claims upon the United States. But it was necessary that the argument go beyond this to demonstrate the legitimacy of immigrant support of Irish nationalism. Loyalty to Ireland had to be

defended in American terms. One of the first to address himself to
this difficulty was Dr. William James MacNeven, the United
Irishman, who in his *Pieces of Irish History* (1807), the first Irish
apologetical work published in the United States, laid down what
would become a familiar and persuasive argument. "What was
tyranny against the American would necessarily be tyranny
against the Irish," he wrote. "And the resistance [to British rule]
so glorious in one country could not be accounted a crime in the
other."[11] The *Pieces of Irish History,* however, was dedicated
only to the defense of the rebels of '98; later writers would link
American and Irish nationalism in a broader chain of history. In
his compulsive love for Ireland, went the argument, the immigrant was only intensifying his Americanism, for Ireland struggled for democracy. "The cause of America in 1776 is the cause of
Ireland in 1876," declared the *Irish World.*

The work of justification and uplift, however, was not confined
to an examination of the Irish in the American past nor to the
moral and political aspirations shared by Ireland and the United
States. It went beyond these considerations or rather included
them in the grandly romantic conception of the Irish as Celts.
The Irish Irish and the Irish of the diaspora were bound together
by this racial tie which was all-important for the future of America. For one of the Celt's special missions was to protect the
Declaration of Independence against "derogation by the Anglo-
Saxon Ascendancy."[12] The struggle for human freedom, which
bound together the destinies of Ireland and the United States,
was, in truth, an aspect of the epic struggle of the Celt against
the Saxon.

Modern awareness of the Celt is not much older than the publication in 1762 of Macpherson's *Fingal,* which made the melan-
choly Celt of the young Scot's imagination a familiar figure to the
reading public of Goethe's Europe. Not, however, until after
Thomas Davis employed the term "Celt" as a pseudonym in the
Dublin *Nation* did it become a militant symbol for Irish nationalists. In response to the already elaborate Anglo-Saxon interpreta-

tion of history, the Irish-Americans brought forth a Celtic version. Lacking historians and publicists of the caliber of Edward Augustus Freeman, James Anthony Froude, and Goldwyn Smith, they were forced to fall back upon the studies in ancient Irish history and literature by Eugene O'Curry, John O'Donovan, and W. K. Sullivan. The immigrant press also drew upon such eccentric enthusiasts as Martin O'Brennan, who believed Celtic was the speech of the Garden of Eden.

Thomas D'Arcy McGee made use of the Celtic Myth in ways that anticipated the Irish literary renaissance at the end of the century. Having caught the Celtic fire from the *Nation* and made researches in the British Museum, he saw in the Celt a being spiritually superior to the materialistic Saxon. Deeply concerned about the influences of the American environment upon Irish family life and morals, he employed the Myth to establish a vantage point from which American society could be brought under criticism. He hoped to give the immigrant a sense of values that would be proof against assimilation. The Celt, he argued, is "naturally aristocratic and full of veneration. . . . Duty, Death, Eternity are more congenial subjects to the Irish mind than Wealth, Liberty, or Fame."[13]

His gratuitous assumption of Celtic spirituality, later reinforced by the speculations of Matthew Arnold and others, would survive as a minor though not unimportant note in Irish-American life. When hard pressed, Irish-American apologists could always fall back upon their spiritual superiority. But on the whole the American Celts had little use for the dreamy and ineffectual people described in Arnold's *Study of Celtic Literature*. The virtues they claimed for their "race" seemed typically American. Not uniqueness and magic, but the earthy ability to get along with people of diverse origins was the special quality of the Celt. They attributed to the ancient Irish people the very achievements that Freeman and his American counterpart, Herbert Baxter Adams of Johns Hopkins University reserved for the Germanic tribes. The origins of democratic institutions, which these historians traced back to the "tun" of the dark German forests, the Celtophiles found on the sunny slopes of Tara. Representative government, trial by jury, and popular education were among the gifts tendered the modern world by the Celts of Ireland.

The American Irish were aware that they were insisting upon Celtic particularism at a time when philologists were asserting a common Aryan origin for Saxon and Celt. There was, too, a certain embarrassment in the fact that very old and distinguished Gaelic families like the Cavanaghs belonged to members of the anti-nationalist Irish gentry, while Celtic partisans bore names obviously Saxon or Norman in origin. Nevertheless, the Celtic Myth served as a useful defensive weapon in the fight against American Saxons at a time when it was fashionable to describe the United States as a Protestant Anglo-Saxon nation. Most Irishmen held to the belief that out of the melting pot would emerge an entirely new people. But as long as others insisted that American culture was Anglo-Saxon, the Irish were prepared to argue that American foundations rested on the Blarney Stone, not Plymouth Rock.

Interest in the Celtic past inevitably aroused interest in reviving the Irish language. Throughout the United States in the 1870's, Philo-Celtic societies were founded for this purpose. The first was established in Boston in 1873, preceding by some three years the founding of the Dublin Society for the Preservation of the Irish Language. By 1878 there were five societies in New York, and in the following year branches were reported as having been established in over thirteen American and Canadian cities, stretching from Boston to San Francisco. Enthusiasts were delighted to discover that the scattered Irish were learning in the United States the language they had the "misfortune not to have learned at home."

But the number so engaged was very small indeed. The Philo-Celtic clubs, as it turned out, were less interested in the revival of Irish than they were in making a contribution to the propaganda war between Celt and Saxon. During his lecture tour in 1870,

Froude had declared that the "Irish as a nation have done nothing which posterity will not be anxious to forget."[14] The Philo-Celts were anxious to prove him wrong. When T. O'Neill Russell of the Dublin language society came to the United States in 1878, he found the Irish-American press indifferent and even opposed to the language revival. The *Irish World,* whose enthusiasm for the Gaelic had influenced Dubliners as well as New Yorkers, warned the hopeful Russell that it had taken up the language movement in 1871 only to prove to "educated dunces" that Ireland had glorious literature in her native language.

By the end of the 1870's, interest in the language movement had sharply declined. Ten years after its founding the Boston Philo-Celtic society reframed its constitution so as to relieve members of the labor of learning Irish. It continued to insist, however, that the cultivation of the Irish or Celtic language and the publication of Irish or Celtic literature was the only way to "vindicate the character of the Irish as a race, from the foul slanders heaped upon them for centuries by English or Anglo-Saxon writers. . . ."[15]

The American Irish used the Celtic Myth to disarm their detractors and give their people hope for the future by fostering pride in the past. But in their hands the Myth developed a more specifically American orientation. It provided the Irish, no matter how far removed in time and place from Ireland, with an image of themselves that justified support of the nationalist movement in the Old Country. The Celtic Myth was also reshaped so as to give expression to those democratic ideals which bound the immigrant Irish closer to the whole American community.

Perhaps the greatest difficulty which confronts the historian of the Irish is that of differentiating between the specifically Irish and specifically Catholic aspects of their lives. They had emerged into the modern world from a past in which Catholicism had played perhaps a stronger role than among any other people of Western Europe. By the end of the seventeenth century, the Irish were a conquered people, their leaders had either fled or been despoiled, and thereafter Gaelic cultural disintegration matched strides with the expansion of English authority. The peasant Irish, therefore, found their securities in the Church and their leadership in the priesthood. Hatred and fear of English Protestantism were part of their cultural heritage.

The essential task confronting nationalists was to make a modern nation out of peoples, Protestant and Catholic, whose historic memories fostered a mutual hostility. Each religious group tended to identify the emergent Irish nation in terms of itself. It was the Protestant nation that led the struggle for political and constitutional reform at the end of the eighteenth century. It was the Catholic nation, under Daniel O'Connell's leadership, that fought and won Catholic emancipation and led the movement for repeal of the Act of Union. Thereafter, Irish nationalism became increasingly identified with the once-slave nation of Catholics.

In the United States, too, the identification of Irish nationalism with Catholicism became increasingly marked. Before the midnineteenth century the term Irish had included the immigrants from Ulster (originally Presbyterian, later, on the frontier, Baptist and Methodist) as well as Catholics from Southern Ireland. Only rarely was any distinction between the two made. But with the floods of impoverished Catholics after the 1840's, the Ulster Irish took to calling themselves Scotch-Irish to make it clear to all Americans that in religion, culture, and capacity for assimilation into American life they were very different human beings from the turbulent Southern Irish.

American Catholics not of Irish origins found it difficult to resist the ready identification of Catholic with Irish. Many of them were as distressed by the appearance of the ragged Irish as were the nativists. But the furious and indiscriminate attack of the Know Nothings made it perilous for the non-Irish Catholics to attempt a distinction between what they considered justifiable criticism of Irish culture and unjustifiable criticism of the Catholic faith. When Orestes Brownson, a convert of whom the American Catholic Church was very proud, made such an effort in 1854 he was promptly howled down by the Irish-Catholic press.

Nevertheless, Irish nationalism and Irish Catholicism involved very different states of mind, different ways of looking at the past and the future. To the Catholic mind the fabled troubles of Ireland were part of a great religious drama, a long martyrdom permitted by God in order to spread His Word. Aware that the emigrating Irish were carrying Catholicism everywhere throughout the English-speaking world, many churchmen saw in that tattered figure an arm of the Lord and in the famines that sent him forth the mysterious "logic of God."

The nationalist called this fatalism. England, both Catholic and Protestant England, was responsible for Ireland's troubles. Irish history was, in their view, the unrelenting struggle of a heroic people for national independence. Foremost in the nationalist martyrology were many Protestants and others like Wolfe Tone who were from the Catholic viewpoint anything but saints. "Wolfe Tone and the men of '98 were fully imbued with the French infidelity of their age," declared McGee's *American Celt*.

The nationalist easily identified himself with American secular ideals, so closely did they conform to the expectations he held for Ireland. But the cleric, seeing Jacobinism in democracy and Protestantism as the mainspring of American society, was full of fears.

With the decline of Know Nothingism, the clergy lost their place as foremost spokesmen for the Irish. Archbishop Hughes' personal influence remained very great until his death in 1863, but the rapid growth of Fenianism in the years immediately following revealed the limitations of clerical influence over the immigrant community. No churchman in the age of Grover Cleveland was as powerful as Hughes had been. James Cardinal Gibbons, Archbishop of Baltimore, is justly celebrated for prudent statesmanship in the all-important post-Civil War years. But his influence was largely negative and felt most directly within the ecclesiastical structure of the Church. Again and again he counseled his fellow bishops not to take action that would tend to alienate Irish-Americans from the Faith.

Few nationalists, of course, desired a break with the Church. They understood its place in Irish life and were themselves, for the most part, more or less practicing Catholics. They were drawn from the same class as the priests and like them had their minds fixed on a transcendent ideal to which they would ruthlessly subordinate friendship and all other lesser matters. (It is striking to find in the letters of Bishop McQuaid of Rochester, for example, the same harsh tone toward antagonists and the same preoccupation with power that one finds in the voluminous letters of John Devoy.) Sharing to a considerable extent the same point of view but responsive to different allegiances, the nationalist and the churchman lived together within the Irish-American community in a state of uneasy tension.

The Irish-American press was the chief instrument of nationalist influence. Newspapers in Ireland were largely irrelevant to the fixed life of the peasantry. To the uprooted Irish of America they were all but a necessity. The newspaper brought them news of home, of ship sailings and arrivals, of relatives missing, and job opportunities available. It taught them the customs and manners of the bourgeois America and was their champion in a sometimes hostile society. It was to the newspaper that the immigrants turned when in their newly awakened consciousness they sought knowledge of Ireland and the Irish.

Not until the 1840's was the Irish immigrant newspaper assured of a secure position. The immigrant flood of the 1840's provided the Irish-American press with readers and the nativist movement gave it a cause. The defeat of Young Ireland at Ballingarry made talent available. Thereafter, a gifted young man could always find employment and opportunity for expression on an immigrant journal. Thomas D'Arcy McGee was a Boston *Pilot* editor at the age of nineteen, and John Boyle O'Reilly was editor and owner of the same paper, the most widely influential of its kind, within ten years after being employed.

The decline of clerical influence in secular affairs and the development of a national body of readers (most major Irish papers in the period 1870–90 had a national circulation) rendered the Irish journal independent of the kind of pressure Archbishop Hughes placed upon McGee and Mitchel. New York was the chief center of Irish-American publishing in the 1880's, with five weeklies designed almost exclusively for immigrant consumption. But every important Irish center supported at least one weekly, and newspapers such as the Boston *Globe* and New York *Herald* gave considerable coverage to Irish nationalist news.

Irish-American nationalism was riddled with ambiguities. An independent Ireland was the goal it pursued. But this was, after all, a remote possibility, a dream. Irish-American societies dedicated to this dream, however, were not at all remote. They were living realities, of consequence in American life. To all they offered companionship and to some, business and political opportunities. They could transform a nobody into a somebody. In the minds of their members, therefore, these organizations tended to assume a greater importance than the pursuit of Irish freedom. Ends and means got confused.

The history of the Fenian movement illustrates the point. The name Fenian derives from the *Fianna*, that ancient warrior band whose exploits under Fionn Mac Cumhaill make up the second cycle of Irish mythology. John O'Mahoney, a Young Ireland exile and a romantic, founded the organization in 1858. The sister organization, led by an artful conspirator, James Stephens, preferred the less mystical name of the Irish Revolutionary Brotherhood. Fenian membership rapidly expanded during the American Civil War. Irishmen trained in both the Union and the Confederate armies joined with the intention of employing their newly learned skills to drive the British out of Ireland. First organized as a series of secret cells, led by a Head Center, in the conventional way of European revolutionary societies, the Brotherhood soon began to reflect its American environment.

At a convention in Philadelphia in 1865, the office of Head

Center was abolished. The new constitution called for a President and a General Congress. The latter, made up of a Senate and a House of Delegates, was invested with all legislative powers; it also elected the President. Authority to originate all money bills was given to the Senate and also the responsibility of approving cabinet appointments.

With a government roughly modeled upon that of the United States, the Fenian Brotherhood conducted itself as an important international power. From the Fenian capitol in the old Moffat mansion opposite Union Square, New York City, flew the Fenian flag of the harp and sunburst. There an army was raised, letters of marque and reprisal were issued, and affairs with other powers were carried on.

A few months after the Philadelphia convention, the Fenian Senate deposed O'Mahoney as President, but he refused to step aside and organized his own faction. "Cut and hack the rotten branches around you," he was advised by Stephens, who was infuriated by the Americanization of the movement. Nevertheless, the Senate Wing, as the anti-O'Mahoney group was called, was the more popular of the two with Irish-Americans.

The Fenians had originally intended to support an uprising in Ireland with an invasion launched from the United States. But faction fighting, to say nothing of the inherent difficulties, prevented them from making more than a token effort. Only a handful of daring men from the United States took part in the abortive Irish rising in 1867.

Canada was closer and in many ways a more attractive target than Ireland. Relations between the United States and Britain were dangerously tense following the Civil War. A number of influential Americans thought Canada should be annexed to the United States in compensation for British aid to the Confederacy. William R. Roberts, a wealthy dry-goods merchant, who headed the Senate Wing, shared this view and apparently hoped that a Fenian attack upon Canada would bring about war between Britain and the United States—a war in which Irish freedom might be won. An invasion of Canada from Buffalo, New York, and St. Albans, Vermont, was attempted in 1866. Anxious Canadians drove the Fenians back into the arms of American government officials who had made no serious effort to stop the well-publicized expedition. Four years later in June, 1870, a final Fenian raid was made across the St. Albans border. After that disaster, the Fenian movement was all but dead.

The nationalist leaders in Ireland thought all this an American madness, but it suited the needs of American politics. The administrations of both Johnson and Grant tolerated the Fenians because their vote was feared, and the Secretary of State, Seward, thought their pugnacity provided him with a useful weapon in bargaining with the British Foreign Office. In the scramble for power that developed during Reconstruction years the politicians exploited the Fenians, and the Fenians, in turn, did their best to exploit the politicians.

The Brotherhood realized that it could not "wipe out the foul stigma attached to the Irish name" if American politics dominated its deliberations. But the Fenians represented power, and the intrusion of politics was not easy to check. When Fenianism swept into the East in 1864, shrewd young politicians like Patrick Collins joined up, and from then on Fenians were too frequently aspirants for public office. The failure of the final raid upon Canada in 1870 was traced to the reluctance of the Senate to commit the Brotherhood to battle out of fear of destroying its political power.

The Fenians had already lost their hold upon Irish-America when Grant informed his Cabinet in May, 1870, that he would no longer permit them the luxury of the "organization of a Government within the United States."[16] The Brotherhood never had more than 45,000 active members and for most of its existence much fewer than that, but it had the moral support of vastly greater numbers. Over 100,000 persons gathered at the picnic grounds in Jones Woods in the Yorkville section of New York City, in March, 1866, to attend a Fenian rally, despite the intense opposition of Archbishop John McCloskey. The wealthier Irish disliked the movement because it maintained the Irish as "a distinct nationality in the midst of the American population," but mass support came from the urban poor.

The Fenian movement reveals Irish-American nationalism in its finest flowering and full ambiguity. Rooted in the hard life of the immigrant, creator of its own sustaining myths, this peculiar nationalism sought to found its own "government" within the United States. Irish nationalism was its unifying cement and the establishment of Irish freedom an important purpose. But in fact Irish-American nationalism was directed chiefly toward American, not Irish, ends. A free Ireland would reflect glory on the Fenians, but of more immediate and practical value was use of the Brotherhood as an American pressure group. Herein lies the explanation for the curious frailty of the bellicose Fenian Brotherhood and the organizations that succeeded it. As long as they remained close to the warming sun of Irish nationalism they thrived; but when by the very law of their being they came into contact with the divisive realities of American life they inevitably disintegrated.

However strange their behavior, the Fenians left their mark on history. English policy in Ireland, complained a member of the House of Commons during the Fenian terror, has formed "a new Irish nation on the other side of the Atlantic, recast in the mould of Democracy, watching for an opportunity to strike a blow at the heart of the Empire." The military character of the Fenian threat stemmed from the experience of the Civil War. The more telling blows that would come in the 1880's derived from the radical social thought engendered in Irish-America by the depression of the 1870's.

O workmen dear, and would you hear
Why do you idle stand,
And why the hum of industry
Is dead throughout the land

There's a cruel band of robbers
Worse than ever yet was known,
Who are filching from us all we earn
And claiming it their own.

Verses from a greenback song,
set to the tune of "The Wearing of the Green"

What is the good of having a republic unless the mass of the
people are better off than in a monarchy? Does not a real
republic mean that all men have an equal chance and not mil-
lions born to suffering and poverty?

The Boston *Pilot*, November 2, 1878

CHAPTER THREE

The Great Depression:

A Search for Social Justice

THE Fenian movement in the United States was a product,
or by-product, of the Civil War, wherein so many Irishmen learned the military arts. But its grotesqueries, one
guesses, sprang more directly from the humiliation suffered before the war. The Fenians expressed acutely the mood of alienation characteristic of the Famine Irish. Though their actions were
deeply influenced by their American experience and ambitions,
there was little—aside from their Anglophobia and perhaps their
Canadian ambitions—with which an American could identify
himself. The Land and National Leagues, however, which in the
1880's succeeded Fenianism, embodied humanitarian and constitutional ideas congenial to the American heart. These organizations bore witness to Irish-America's absorption of the American spirit, its acceptance of the American proposition once so
scornfully rejected. The Irish in the Gilded Age, as Van Wyck
Brooks said of John Boyle O'Reilly, evoked for many Americans
poignant memories of their own prewar idealism.

The war brought change. By sharing in its agonies, for whatever the reasons and however much against the will, the Irish
participated intimately in the American people's most terrible experience. Meagher's Irish Brigade at Antietam's Bloody Lane, its

43

foolish gallantry at Marye's Heights behind Fredericksburg, the exploits of the Irish Massachusetts 9th Regiment, the Illinois 19th, and the gallant 69th of New York became in later years part of the legend. (In an extraordinary act of courtesy, the New York Draft Riots were all but forgotten.) As the Irish were absorbed into the Civil War legend, so too they absorbed the mythic evaluations later generations would place upon the war. In retrospect, it was fought to end slavery and extend the domain of human freedom, and the Irish like other Americans became postwar Abolitionists. It was an important commitment. Not that it wiped out Irish distrust of do-gooders, but it did make it possible for more generous impulses to flow. As we shall see, when the Irish made their own fight in the 1880's they did so in the language and with the idealism of pre–Civil War reformers.

Perhaps all this would have happened in its own way without the war. American life after all had a meaning for the second and third generation, the sons and grandsons of Famine immigrants, that was hidden from their forebears. What could be more meaningful to the young and ambitious poor, bearing within themselves the memory of old insults, than a myth which declared that all men are created equal and yet that each should strive to better himself? Without the softened attitudes toward the Irish which the war generated, however, it would have been very difficult for the second- and third-generation Irish Catholic to speak his mind. A repetition of the intense religious conflicts of the 1850's would have muzzled them as D'Arcy McGee had been muzzled. But in the Gilded Age the liberals were popular figures: Patrick Ford, John Boyle O'Reilly, and John Ireland, Archbishop of St. Paul, the ecclesiastical spokesman for American individualism. These champions were able to make their voices heard, though not without a fight from the numerically superior conservatives among the Irish-Americans.

While American prejudice against the Irish had softened, it had not by any means disappeared. Throughout most of the Gilded Age, the Hibernians were looked upon as a more or less perma-

nent servant force. Americans had borrowed from English literature two stereotypes that, while hardly flattering to the Irish,
were nevertheless free of venom: Paddy, the hapless, witty Irishman, given to drink and quick to tears and laughter, who loved
nothing more than "rows and ructions"; and Bridget, the chaste
and prudent but comically ignorant serving girl. Paddy and
Bridget were disorderly but funny, Irish but thoroughly attached
to the Stars and Stripes.

Out of these stereotypes Ned Harrigan and Tony Hart (Harrigan and Hart) contrived to make a unique art with their famous
productions at the Theatre Comique in the 1880's. To judge from
his affection for the *Mulligan Guards* and other Harrigan and
Hart plays, the ordinary Irishman enjoyed the role in which he
was cast. As for the ordinary middle-class American, he too enjoyed the productions. They confirmed what he wanted to believe.

The stereotype Paddy was not without its truths. The Irish did
love a row, were too often found with drink taken, and did rule
over the low life of American cities. But this stereotype and the
accommodation it sustained failed to reflect the changing realities
of Irish-American life. The ragged and comic-appearing immigrant in the 1880's was giving way to the solemn, ambitious
second-generation Irish-American who was knocking at the gates
of the political parties, the professions, and business. Even Irish
delinquencies made for change. The Irish love of whisky, after
all, raised up a prosperous class of brewers and saloon keepers
like Patrick J. Kennedy of Boston, the grandfather of John F.
Kennedy. And Irish love of physical combat bred several generations of famous athletes who established the very American tradition that sport was a ladder upward. The painfully serious James
J. Corbett, who at New Orleans in 1892 defeated John L. Sullivan
for the heavyweight boxing championship, wanted above all
things to be considered a gentleman. The change is mirrored in
the themes of Harrigan and Hart. Harrigan's last great hit (Hart
having died in 1888) was *Reilly and the Four Hundred*, pro-

duced in 1890. Reilly is no Handy Andy servant type but a parvenu pawnbroker with a socially ambitious wife. In the hit song, "Maggie Murphy's Home,"

There's an organ in the parlor to give the place a tone
And you're welcome every evening at Maggie Murphy's home.

As the 1880's wore on and the knocking grew louder and more insistent, anti-Irish feeling proportionately increased, but at no time did anything so menacing as the Know Nothings emerge.

The temper of the Irish-American community struck contemporaries as highly inflamed. In retrospect it is clear that behind Irish radical rhetoric were fundamentally conservative demands. The authentic rebel note was sounded when they demanded equal rights for all and attacked the citadels of privilege in business and politics. But mostly the Irish wanted to be middle-class and respectable. Behind the flaming intransigence of the Irish nationalist (or for that matter behind the thundering of Populist and Socialist) there was nine times out of ten an ambitious Horatio Alger figure. Consider handsome Patrick Collins: a labor organizer and Fenian in the 1860's, in 1881 the second president of the American Land League, thereafter a member of Congress, Consul General at London, and Boston's Mayor from 1901 until his death in 1905. Proper Bostonians today remember him as "Good Mayor Collins." In this career there was no betrayal. In the Lace Curtain Irishman the rebel found fulfillment. But in the Gilded Age it was the rebel note that most forcibly struck contemporaries. Whether laborer or lawyer, the Irish were not content, and they were knocking at the gates.

Irish discontent was given new force and focus by the depression that began when Jay Cooke's banking house failed in 1873. Occupying the marginal jobs in most industries, the Irish were hard hit. They filled the bread lines and clamored for work. Some became desperate. In 1877 the railway employees of four great eastern trunk lines, of whom about one-third were Irish, went out on strike when wages were arbitrarily cut by 10 per cent. The strikes snaked across the nation. The citizens of Baltimore, Pittsburgh, Chicago, and San Francisco were terrified as violent attacks were made upon railroad property. "Hell is open and the lid is off," announced the New York *Sun*. President Hayes sent federal troops into Pennsylvania to put down the violence.

Irish violence was at its most spectacular in the anthracite coal country of northeastern Pennsylvania. In those rugged hills the Irish confronted their ancient antagonists, the Welsh, the Scots, and the English; and terrorism was an old story. With the coming of hard times, brawling in the saloons and shootings in the streets increased alarmingly. Nine men were murdered in the years 1874 and 1875. Pinkerton detectives hired by Franklin B. Gowen of the Reading Railroad, whose operations dominated the region, traced most of these murders to the Molly Maguires, a secret faction operating within the local lodges of the Ancient Order of Hibernians. On June 21, 1877, ten Molly Maguire members were hanged for their crimes.

Like the Mafia of today, the Molly Maguires were endowed by the inflamed imagination of their contemporaries with a more elaborate organization than they possessed, and they were probably accused of more crimes than they committed. Nevertheless, the terror was real enough, and it followed the pattern of agrarian crime in Ireland. Crude threatening notices bearing sketches of coffins, night burnings and ambushes, and witnesses who would not testify against their own made up the pattern. Ethnic and religious hatreds blended with economic grievances, for the English and the Welsh were the bosses of the coal fields. Inevitably, the terrorist leaders sought to make political capital out of their power to intimidate. From our perspective the Molly leaders were labor racketeers, but in the eyes of sympathetic contemporaries they were honest if desperate workers driven to terrorism in order to control the price of labor just as in Ireland the peasants were driven to Whiteboyism to control the price of rents.[1]

In California, Irish desperation found still another outlet. California's business depression had been exacerbated by the collapse of the previous decade's mining boom. Disillusioned miners tramping into San Francisco swelled the army of unemployed. Their ragged poverty contrasted vividly, as Henry George noted, with the garish mansions of the mining rich on Nob Hill. News in July, 1877, of the great railroad strike electrified the city's poor. Thousands gathered on the sandlots before the newly constructed city hall to vent their anger against the Southern and Central Pacific railroads, which controlled the state.

The mob, however, quickly found its scapegoat in the Chinese, whose willingness to work for low wages was popularly regarded as the source of California unemployment. Thereafter the slogan "The Chinese Must Go" became the rallying cry of San Francisco's unhappy people. Many Irishmen took part in the movement, but none achieved so great a notoriety as Denis Kearney, the orator of the sandlots. Born in Ireland in 1847, the worst year of the Great Famine, this thick-headed Irishman had been a sailor and in 1877 was a drayman.

Kearney and his Irish followers were caught in the classic dilemma of the minority group. In the name of their rights, they were forced to deny the rights of others. Brought in by the business community to serve as cheap labor in competition with the Irish, the Orientals were defended by the local Protestant clergy who were as much anti-Irish as they were pro-Chinese.

For a time, Kearney was a power in California politics, leading the Workingmen's Party into frenzied agitation against the Chinese. He was repeatedly arrested by the city authorities, only to emerge more popular than ever. His head thoroughly turned, he came East in 1878 to harangue the Irish of Boston and New York. He assured them that the Chinese lived "on rice and rats" and menaced the American workingman. He was one of the first Irishmen—though certainly not the last—to relieve his own miseries by persecuting others. His campaign found a response among the eastern Irish and made American liberals speculate complacently on the facility with which Irishmen adopted the style of Know Nothings.[2]

The violence of these days shocked the Irish-American community. Belief that the Pennsylvania Mollys were fighting the old battle in the old way drove thoughtful Irishmen into a search for a new understanding of their predicament. The old nationalist sentimentalities that had long served as a substitute for thought were abandoned or put aside. The *Irish World* called for a new realism. St. Patrick's Day nonsense, with its rhetoric about Ireland's golden age (Malachi's Collar of Gold and all that), O'Connell's blarney, and Young Ireland's vaporings about the national soul had all been a disservice. They had not been instructive in what the depression had made so manifest—that free institutions were worthless unless based upon a just economic and social order. "Let Irish revolutionaries take notice. It won't be enough to sever the 'golden link of the crown.' The founders of our republic did that, and yet labor languishes and business suffers." No longer did American history appear to be simply the chronicle of a nation's march to greatness. Something had gone wrong.

In the search for that something, the Irish-American press brought American society under severe criticism, but it was Jeffersonian thought they employed for the purpose. In this work Patrick Ford played a leading part. Two great social evils, he believed, had made a mockery of American democracy: the immorality of taking interest for the use of money, and rent for the use of land.

Ford learned about the evils of interest chiefly from the Greenback monetary reformers whose proposals outraged conservatives in the years following the Civil War. The greenbackers asserted that money, being a public medium of exchange, should be under the exclusive control of the national government and that interest rates should be governed solely by the annual increase in national wealth, thus reflecting the creativity of labor which alone conferred property rights. Applied to the thorny monetary problems inherited from the war, these were explosive principles. Bankers and other holders of the public debt wanted the legal tender notes (greenbacks) issued during the war taken out of circulation and the war bonds—purchased with depreciated greenbacks—

redeemed in gold. Greenback principles, however, called for retaining the greenbacks as the sole national currency, making them interconvertible with the bonds, the interest rates of which would be set very low. Thus the "money monopolist" would be thwarted. "This was a plan," said the pompous Senator George Frisbie Hoar of the Bay State, "which Massachusetts has pronounced a scheme of dishonesty and infamy in every way that her sentiment could be made known."³

Ford was a dedicated greenbacker. When old Peter Cooper ran for president on the Greenback ticket in 1876, Ford served on the party's New York State central committee. Two years later a thousand throw-away copies of the *Irish World* were distributed among the voters of Rockland, Maine, in support of a Greenback-Labor candidate. As late as 1881, when the cause was dying, Ford remained faithful.

It seems probable, however, that he was never entirely satisfied with the Greenback program, which under the influence of its farm supporters became more blatantly inflationist. He had a higher end in view than the propagation of cheap money. He wanted to abolish usury, against which Scripture and justice cried out, and the "money interest" which it supported. The latter was a monster which he and his fellows regarded with almost superstitious fascination. "The gold ring is like a huge boa constrictor. . . . It has wound itself about the nation, crushing its bones and sucking the life blood from the heart."⁴ The monster robbed the farmer and the manufacturer of the fruits of their enterprise and the laborer of his reward. It was the money power that mocked democracy and unleashed violence upon the nation.

But this was not the only and not the greatest threat to American life. Riches gained from land rents were even more destructive. And for his Irish readers, only a generation or so removed from the fabled green fields, the proposition that the greatest social evil flowed from the private monopoly of land was especially persuasive. The land theory like the monetary derived from eighteenth century natural rights thought. Land, air, and water belonged to all. No one could be denied access to any of them. They could not be the subject of individual expropriation because they were created by the hand of God and not by the labor of man. To expropriate what belonged to God was sinful. The land, as the *Irish World* thundered out week after week, belonged to God and His people.

For land reform propaganda the *Irish World* editor rummaged among the books of social concern that the nineteenth-century Industrial Revolution had generated. Louis Blanc, William Cobbett, John Stuart Mill, John Bright, and Thomas Carlyle were among the writers called upon to testify. Thomas Spence, the late eighteenth-century Newcastle-on-Tyne precursor of Henry George, merited "a high place in heaven for domesticating the thought of Tom Jefferson." *Irish World* readers were made familiar with George and the Land Reform League of California long before the publication of *Progress and Poverty*.

Ford's concern about land monopoly was widely shared. Among greenbackers and other dissidents, dissatisfaction with the Homestead Act (1862) was intense. Instead of providing the poor with western lands, the act had worked to the advantage of land speculators. The mammoth wheat farms of the High Plains and the vast landholdings of the railroads appeared to testify to the impotence of the Homestead legislation. In the hope of still making the West a haven for the poor and a sanctuary for the independent small farmer, Ford supported the Irish Catholic Benevolent Union's western colonizing efforts and joined with other reformers in calling for government subsidies to homesteaders. In June, 1878, Benjamin ("Beast") Butler, the scourge of Massachusetts' orthodoxy, introduced such a bill in Congress, but nothing came of it.[5] Congress was committed to plutocracy and *laissez faire*.

The hard times, the violence in the streets, and the indifference manifested by the state and central governments to their demands convinced these reformers that a revolutionary crisis was at hand. Said the *Irish World* on October 13, 1877:

The mad Scotts, and Vanderbilts, and Gowens, the railroad lords and coal-mine lords, and the banks and all the mad multitudes of pettier monopolists, have drawn up their new plan of a land, mine, and money oligarchy. . . . its ruffian press shouts: "Shoot! Slay! Here one rioter was shot where hundreds should have filled the ground." What a howl that bloodhound press would raise if we should advise that the mad monopolists . . . be shot down in the same way.

Like James Fintan Lalor in 1847, Ford in 1877 believed that the social order was close to dissolution, the social compact all but broken. In the crisis Irish news was pushed aside to make room for the writings of reformers and theorists of varying convictions. Socialists like Philip Van Patten, national secretary of the Socialist Labor party, and P. J. McGuire, future co-founder of the American Federation of Labor, engaged in learned wrangles with J. K. Ingalls, Henry Appleton, and other extreme individualists whose ideas derived from the radical strain of Jeffersonian thought. Ford considered it a "sacred duty" to encourage the dialogue, although his own convictions clearly lay with the individualists.

The impending crisis of which he was both prophet and propagandist was not in his view the Marxist day of judgment, which would pit the proletariat against the *bourgeoisie*. It was that other struggle, fought and won for Americans in earlier times by Jefferson and Jackson, between the producers of wealth—the farmers, laborers, and small businessmen—and the parasitical capitalist, who expropriated gigantic wealth without commensurate labor. At stake was the natural right of all to the rewards of individual effort.

The Depression of 1873 also moved John Boyle O'Reilly's Boston *Pilot* to the left as considerations of social justice became more urgent than the paper's traditional religious and ethnic concerns. Like Ford, O'Reilly saw the problems of capital and labor in essentially Jeffersonian terms.

What is the good of having a republic unless the mass of the people are better off than in a monarchy? Does not a real republic mean that all men have an equal chance and not millions born to suffering and poverty?

The same questions were asked in O'Reilly's novel, *Moondyne* (1880), a work that drew upon his Australian prison experiences and that went through twelve editions. In his poems, "From the Earth, a Cry," and "City Streets," he left no doubt about his sympathy for the oppressed and his condemnation of institutions in which "progress and property rank over man." The *Pilot* was a tireless critic of the new monopolies and their plutocratic masters. It supported the Greenback Movement, though it worried about the consequences of inflation upon the wage earner. And it joined Ford in calling for government subsidies to homesteaders.

But in the well-ordered pages of the *Pilot* there was no place for the incendiary language of a Patrick Ford or Denis Kearney. O'Reilly lacked the radical temperament. Beneath the romanticism that he displayed like an actor's cloak, he was essentially a man of prudence, devoid of Ford's dogmatism, indifferent to intellectual theorizing and consistency. During his lifetime he was sympathetic to a host of reformers of the most diverse persuasions. He felt a deep pity for the poor, and a sense of compassion appears to have been what he valued most in a reformer. He deplored, as he wrote in a memorable line, "charity scrimped and iced, in the name of a cautious, statistical Christ."

Both Ford and O'Reilly, despite their very different personal styles, were engaged in educating the immigrant in the values of American liberal thought and in adapting its traditions to his needs. To these champions of a rising people, liberalism offered an exciting and generous creed. Nevertheless, we would deceive ourselves were we to take their words too literally. Their fight against monopoly appears by their writings to have been a titanic struggle against demons—Gould, Vanderbilt, Armour, and the rest —with the entire American industrial system at stake. But this might better be understood as evidence of Irish frustration, which demanded a demonology, than of Irish objectives. (Perhaps, too, in some cases it reveals the intoxication words had for a newly literate people. Kearney, who learned public speaking in San Francisco's Lyceum of Culture, obviously enjoyed calling his antagonists "slimy imps of hell.") Most of the Irish champions actually aimed at achieving more humble things: more and better municipal jobs, especially on the police and fire departments; political nominations and appointments; equality of consideration for Catholicism in the Protestant-dominated public institutions—schools, hospitals, orphan asylums, and prisons. For most Irish radicals these concrete objectives were more important than their Jeffersonian wrappings. Patrick Ford appears to have been one of the few prominent enthusiasts for the Greenback-Labor program who rigorously insisted upon implementing its principles in all their purity. But even he, within a few years, would find it not unpleasant to mingle on terms of intimacy with the monopolists within the Republican party.

The Greenback-Labor party represented a theory but it was also a force. It promised to break down the walls of privilege. This was especially true in Massachusetts, where that old adventurer, Ben Butler, was the Greenback champion. Having lost his once-great influence in the Republican party, Butler in 1878 and 1879 ran for governor of the Bay State as an irregular Democrat after failing to bully the regular organization into supporting his candidacy. In these campaigns he had the backing of the greenbackers, plentiful in the textile and shoe towns of the state, and of many Irish. The *Pilot,* which had once called him an "amiable kleptomaniac," described his 1878 campaign as a fight of the people against the "office-holders, ring commissions, capitalists, corporations, and politicians."[6]

Though the Lowell politician lost on both these occasions, he demonstrated that he was the state's strongest Democrat. The conservative Democratic leaders bearing their Brahmin names—Judge Abbott, Leverett Saltonstall—were persuaded, therefore, to come to terms with him. In 1881 he received the regular Democratic nomination and won an overwhelming victory, piling up the largest majority that any Democratic candidate for state or national office would compile in that decade. He made, however, a very poor governor. So scandalous was his performance (he devoted much of his time trying to prove that a state hospital made a good thing out of the high mortality rate among its infant wards by selling the bodies to Harvard Medical School) that Harvard University broke with tradition and refused to offer him an honorary degree.

It has always been an embarrassment to the admirers of John Boyle O'Reilly that he was a friend and supporter of Butler, whose shenanigans remind one of the late Senator Joseph McCarthy. "He possessed a singular capacity for throwing the House into a turmoil of disputation," wrote James G. Blaine of the irrepressible Butler's congressional career. He was attractive to the Irish for a number of reasons. A once-poor Yankee boy who had become a wealthy lawyer and textile manufacturer, Butler was never able to rid himself of the mucker's envy of the respectable classes. He bore his resentments conspicuously like a badge. The Irish delighted in his attacks upon the "great idol Respectability" and in the wit with which he exposed the hypocritical solemnities of the Senator Hoars. They identified themselves with him.

> We Irish who have been preached down; howled down throughout civilization should after our terrible experience be able to meet our enemy at every turn. What public man in America has ever undergone such a swish of filthy abuse as General Butler . . . and his enemies are our enemies. . . .[7]

Moreover, though he made a mockery of Greenback theory, Butler was a genuine revolutionary force in Bay State life. He helped refashion the Democratic party in Massachusetts to the advantage of the Irish. Two years after he stepped down as governor in 1883, the Irish elected Hugh O'Brien to be Boston's first Irish Catholic mayor. Butler offered the Massachusetts Irish that equal chance for which O'Reilly and generations of Americans before him believed the Republic had been established.

In New York the Tammany organization was too strong and

too well connected with the rank-and-file Irish to be vulnerable to a Butler-like attack. Indeed, the politically ambitious New York Irishmen had no need of a maverick like Butler. The Irish were already established and were on their way to becoming the monopolists of New York politics. Irish reformers and nationalists like Patrick Ford detested Tammany as much as anyone. But not until 1886, when Henry George ran for mayor, would they have a champion who could offer a serious challenge to the Tiger.

The rise of Irish-American radicalism split the Catholic community. Ecclesiastics were dismayed by the secret societies—the Clan na Gael, the Knights of Labor, and others—which their flocks were joining. The Molly Maguires had revealed once again the terrible dangers of tolerating secret societies. Conservatives were dismayed also by the Irish interest in social thought not sanctioned by the Church. James McMaster, the sharp-tongued and ultramontane editor of the New York *Freeman's Journal,* made a fierce attack upon John Boyle O'Reilly. The novel *Moondyne,* he said, was paganism.

Denis Kearney's activities brought him to the attention of the Archbishop of San Francisco, Joseph S. Alemany. In an interview granted the agitator, the cleric is alleged to have accused him of being a bad, communistic Catholic. "I am, your reverence, and maybe a better Catholic than yourself," Kearney was reported to have answered.

> I am on the side of the poor and oppressed, as the founder of the Church and the apostles were. I speak for the thousands of hungry men, women, and children. You represent $14,000,000 of Church property in this city alone.[8]

Whether or not Kearney answered so boldly, the anti-clericalism he expressed was deepening throughout the decade and would explode in the 1880's in the controversy between the Irish followers of Father Edward McGlynn and Archbishop Corrigan of New York.

The *Irish World* inevitably called forth ecclesiastical fulminations. In 1879 the paper was placed under ban in the diocese of Alton, Illinois, and its teachings denounced by Richard J. Gilmour, the Glasgow-born Bishop of Cleveland, in a pastoral letter that set forth the conservative viewpoint. Inequities in society are inevitable, said the Bishop. "Some men must rise, others must fall; without this there would be no motive for individual push. . . . A man's labor is his own . . . to sell at whatsoever price he pleases. . . . It is no disgrace to be poor. Our master was poor."

Ford replied that the Bishop spoke like an "iron-hearted political economist. . . . in the service of the monopolists, and very unlike a preacher of the word of Him who was the Father of the poor." Justice and Christian love, the editor said, not competition, should govern relations between men.

As for poverty, a little of it goes a long way. "If it is a good thing, why not distribute its blessings around. . . . God loves the poor but he does not love filth and squalor." Land monopoly has defrauded man of "free access to the gratuitous gifts of the Creator, whereby every man will be afforded a chance to work, the fruits of which he may enjoy with his own family under his own vine." In closing, Ford asked a question that troubled many: "Can a man be a good Catholic who believes in the Declaration of Independence?"[9]

Ford was gripped by many of the lunacies that Richard Hofstadter and others have revealed as inherent in the *petit bourgeois* radicalism of the greenbacker and the Populist—an anti-Semitism which derived from his monetary theories and from an almost hallucinatory belief that capitalist societies were held together by a web of conspiracy in which a spiderlike Shylock (Baron de Rothschild) pulled the strings. Nevertheless, he helped keep alive in his own day in the face of conservative Catholic criticism the exalted implications about man and society which are to be found in the Declaration of Independence.

Irish-American radicals argued that land monopolists were as troublesome in the United States as they were in Ireland. They found a ready symbol for this view in James Scully, a notorious Tipperary landlord who, after fighting many a bloody battle with his tenants, emigrated in 1868 to the United States, where he took up great tracts of land in the West and ran into more tenant trouble. But clearly the James Scullys were more of a burden to Ireland than to the United States.

The Irish landlord system had survived the Great Famine ordeal without the substantial improvement many had anticipated. More than half of the 5,412,000 Irish counted in the census of 1870 were tenant farmers or their dependents, and fully five-sixths of the tenants were tenants-at-will, subject to eviction should they fail to pay the rent on "gale day." Though the Land Act of 1870 dismayed the landlords and for a time encouraged the tenant farmer, it did not substantially alter their relations. The peasantry remained without sufficient guarantees that improvements made by them to their holdings would not result in a rent hike, and rack-renting and capricious evictions remained an ever-present threat to the typical post-Famine farmer whose twenty acres or so were too small to support his family. Seasonal work in Great Britain and remittances from a son or a daughter abroad provided his narrow margin of security. The potato, which had so disastrously failed in 1846, supplemented by Indian corn ("stirabout") was still the staple of the Irish diet; the mud-floored hut, not much superior to that of the Congo native, was still the most familiar dwelling of the beautiful Irish country-side.

The Encumbered Estates Act of 1849, which its authors had hoped would bring new capital and efficient farming practices into Ireland, was on the whole a disappointment. The new land-lords whose purchases had been facilitated by the act were chiefly from the Irish business community—shopkeepers, attorneys, and "gombeen men" (village usurers). Possessing little in the way of spare capital, they failed to improve their estates to any significant degree. And those who did invariably ran into difficulties with their tradition-minded tenantry. Only in the exaction of rents were the new owners more efficient than the old.

The presence of these parvenus among the gentry probably diminished the peasantry's customary awe of their betters, thereby laying open the entire landlord class to the fury of the dispossessed. The Earl of Leitrim's murder in 1878 demonstrated that the rural terrorist was no respecter of social status. For decades the Earl had followed the practice of ejecting tenants from his many properties whenever the need for pasture land demanded it. He also had a reputation for exploiting the mystique which surrounded the gentleman from the Big House to seduce the local country girls. He was ambushed on his great estate in Donegal by a group hiding opposite an empty hut from which a widow had recently been evicted. His murderers were never caught. It was said they slipped away to America.

The Irish-American press felt little compulsion to apologize for the Earl's murder. In its judgment the Anglo-Irish had no rights to Irish land. Several hundred years of residence had not earned them prescriptive rights. They were robbers. The people to whom the land belonged were the peasantry. The whole of Ireland, in the opinion of the *Irish World*, should be sliced up into small peasant holdings. The possibility that the peasants themselves might in time become oppressive landlords could be avoided by making "rents for land irrecoverable at law." A concerted refusal to pay rents was the weapon most frequently urged upon the peasantry.

It is strict justice [wrote an Irishman from Leavenworth, Kansas, to the *Irish World*, May 13, 1876] that should be meted out to the whole kindred of exterminators who turn out hundreds of God's children of every age . . . on the roadside to perish in winter. Whether or not freedom from English rule be effected, the landlords might be toppled over by a united determination to pay rents no longer, and to slay without mercy . . . all who endeavored to enforcement or eviction.

In 1879 Ford established a special fund—the Spread the Light Fund—to subsidize shipment of his paper to the British Isles, where the shock waves from the American depression had tumbled agricultural prices and shattered the job market. The Irish in Britain's grimy industrial cities, feeling the pressures that were arousing their countrymen in Boston and Chicago and heirs to the same radical traditions, were receptive to the argument that land monopoly was at the bottom of their troubles.

As the 1870's drew to a close Ford assured his readers everywhere that apocalyptic changes were in the offing. "Even you landlords over there in Ireland must see . . . that your dark blighting shadow cannot hold its place in the sky forever."

Remember, remember the Fifth of November
The comical, chemical plot
When Rossa uprose on his base Saxon foes
And gallantly scumfished the lot.

Scientific and placid, he took osmic acid.
And uncorked the stuff in St. Stephens;
And sure by the powers in under two hours,
Ould Ireland was minus a grievance.

From *Punch*, the English magazine of humor

Now I know some pious people will feel mad and vexed at this
spirit of hate to their much admired England, and will even
curse me as a communistic Irishman! Well, let them, I don't tell
even half the hate I bear them and it in my soul.

Letter from JOHN McCORMAC, *Irish World,*
October 23, 1875

CHAPTER FOUR

Search for a Nation:

Plots and Parliamentarians

W E know that hard times had redirected the thrust of Irish hatreds. Many aspects of American life now came under Irish fire, and disaffection for American plutocracy became a new Irish passion. No longer did England seem unique in cruelty. Nevertheless, John Bull remained the most compelling symbol of Irish frustration. To the residual hatreds fed by famine memories new ones were added which were chargeable to John Bull. To the Irish worker knocking about the country looking for a job, the raw laborer in the Pennsylvania anthracite fields forced to endure Welsh contempt because he lacked Welsh skills, the bitter children of a brutalized, drunken Irish father in Chicago, the ambitious Irish-American lawyer of Omaha who could not get a secure foothold on the next rung up, to all of these and others it seemed that their origins were against them. They were assured by the American Myth that the future was open, but the past was a heavy burden, and the past was England. Lacking money and skills, without even a kitchen culture, the bulk of the Irish were forced, like Jim Tully's father in *Shanty Irish*, to "throw mud with a crooked stick." A letter to the *Irish World* of January 1, 1876, from "Ballaghaslane Beara" of Virginia City, Nevada, spoke for many.

We are slaves in the United States, and . . . the reason for such a state of things is plain: Because we haven't an Irish nation. England defrauded us of the means by which, when leaving Ireland for America, we could afford to settle down on a western farm; and we are therefore chained down to live in the mire of the cities. Secondary reasons may also be put forward, such as . . . the Anglo-American moneyed portion . . . who will not employ an Irishman if they can get somebody else. . . .

The Depression of 1873, as the previous chapter suggested, set forces of social reform in motion within the Irish-American communities, but it also intensified that yearning for a national identity, for an independent Irish nation that would confer dignity upon a degraded people. In the following decade the two forces would clash, splintering the Irish-American community. But that takes us ahead of our story. In the 1870's the nationalists, with whom this chapter is concerned, were devotedly engaged in trying to shape a new organizational basis for the passions of nationalism.

In January, 1871, when the *Cuba* Five arrived and received the tumultuous reception described in the prologue to this work, the United States was strewn with the wreckage of nationalist societies. What had remained of Fenian prestige had been destroyed in late May of the previous year when one final and disastrous effort was made from St. Albans, Vermont, to invade Canada. Nationalists looked forward to the arrival of the *Cuba* Five and other released prisoners in the hope that somehow they could bind up Fenian wounds and make them a power once again. But this was beyond the capacities of any man. Fenianism had become too closely embroiled with American party politics. Most of the released prisoners, having heard of the depravity of Tammany Hall under Boss Tweed, were firm Republicans. Rossa was persuaded to run against Tweed for the New York State senate and was soundly beaten. Democratic Fenians thereupon accused him of peddling nationalism "in the slimy political mar-

ket of America." Devoy had been advised by his old British army
and Fenian comrade, John Boyle O'Reilly, to forget nationalist
politics and get himself a good job. But Devoy chose instead to
pursue what would be his life's work, the development of a reli-
able and tough-minded organization dedicated to overthrowing
British rule in Ireland. After a number of false starts he found a
home in the Clan na Gael.

The Clan na Gael, or United Brotherhood, had been founded
in June, 1867, by Jerome J. Collins, later scientific editor of James
Gordon Bennett's New York *Herald,* and a number of other nationalists anxious to bury Fenian factionalism. Under the direction of Devoy, who held a job on Bennett's *Herald* and rose to
become foreign editor, and Dr. William Carroll, a Philadelphia
physician of Ulster Presbyterian origins and disciple of John
Mitchel, the Clan became, by the end of the 1870's, the single
most powerful Irish revolutionary society in the United States.

The Clan profited from Fenian mistakes. Every effort was
made to avoid the cult of personalities and to maintain secrecy,
whereas the Fenians had been mesmerized by the mystical James
Stephens, and had, under the prodding of the Catholic Church
and their own vanity, abandoned secrecy for publicity. Admission to each Clan camp was by recommendation only and was
accomplished through Masonic-like rites in which, among other
things, the candidate had to profess a belief in God. Camps
elected their officers, known as junior and senior guardians, and
were grouped in districts presided over by district officers. The
latter made up a national executive board, whose chairman was
annually elected. After 1877, a joint revolutionary directory
bound together the Clan and the Irish Republican Brotherhood. It
consisted of seven members, three chosen by the Clan executive,
three by the I.R.B. supreme council, with the seventh man chosen
by the first six. To ensure secrecy of communication, a simple
letter cipher was drawn up which employed the letter of the
alphabet next after the one actually meant. The formal cipher
appears to have been little used, however, (perhaps because it

transformed "Ireland" into "Jsfmboe"), except to lend further mystery to the initiating ceremonies. Substitute names and metaphorical language, chiefly drawn from the business world, were employed in correspondence with sufficient rigor to leave the historian with a number of puzzles. Throughout the 1870's the Clan kept its secrets. In the 1880's its inner life was periodically exposed, as scandals multiplied and its secrets became available to journalists. In the 1890's it provided the humorist Finley Peter Dunne with lots of material.

After a decade of existence the organization had a membership of perhaps 10,000. Working-class Irishmen appear to have made up the Clan rank and file, while leadership was drawn from the middle class, from medicine, law, journalism, and from skilled-trades-unions. Terence V. Powderly, Grand Master Workman of the Knights of Labor and one-time Mayor of Scranton, Pennsylvania, was senior guardian of Camp 470; Senator S. B. Conover, U. S. Senator from Florida, was a member of Carroll's camp. John W. Goff, the Tammany Hall antagonist who won fame as the Lexow Commission counsel in its investigation of New York City police corruption in 1893 and later became a New York State Supreme Court judge, was for a time in the 1870's a Devoy rival for Clan leadership. Troy, New York, had the distinction of being the home of the largest and perhaps most influential city organizations. According to Devoy, the mayor, the chief of police, and the comptroller were all members.

Clan revolutionary strategy was based on the assumption that sooner or later England would be involved in a war that could offer opportunities for an armed uprising in Ireland. From 1875 until the Berlin Conference in the spring of 1878, at which Disraeli arranged with Russia a "peace with honor," war between England and the Russian Empire over the crumbling Turkish power in the Balkans seemed an ever-present possibility. In November, 1876, when Clan hopes for war were high, a Clan delegation, through the good offices of Senator Conover, met with the Russian Ambassador to Washington. The Russian diplomat was graciously informed of the advantages his country would find in an understanding with the revolutionaries of Ireland. The Ambassador was not impressed. He pointed out, in words that were to make a deep impression on Devoy and have consequences for the future, that he saw little public evidence in Ireland of strong nationalist feeling hostile to the British connection.

The search for allies continued. In 1877 the long-projected revolutionary directory was established, ensuring closer cooperation between the Clan's executive directory and the I.R.B. supreme council. Hopes remained high for a Russian alliance and for one with Spain that would hold out to that country the bait of winning Gibraltar. In 1876 an even more daring enterprise was undertaken. The Clan undertook to subsidize the experiments John P. Holland, a County Clare man and former Christian Brother, was making to develop submarines. Some $60,000 was spent in the following five years in building three boats, only the third of which proved sound. (Ultimately, Holland's designs were taken up by the United States Navy. Like so many Clan projects, little of benefit to the Clan was realized and the project left them with interminable financial disputes.) The revolutionaries had hopes that the Fenian rams would sweep the Atlantic clear of British ships. Also in 1876, Carroll urged that plans be laid for the mobilization of 5,000 to 10,000 men to be ready at a month's notice to set off for Ireland.

But mostly they were building castles in the air. The depression had emptied Irish pockets, and money for arms was scarce. The I.R.B. was split by feuds and dominated by John O'Leary and Charles Kickham, literary men both, and vigorous personalities, but hardly capable of carrying out Carroll's fantasies. A somewhat more sober estimate of what might be done was offered by General F. F. Millen, an adventurer and former Fenian who had won his title in the Mexican Army:

Not since the time of the Crimean war and Indian mutiny has there been so propitious a juncture in the affairs of our country. At last, if often repeated reports in the European press are to be believed, England will drift into war with Russia. . . . In 1865, we saw with regret that large sums of money which ought to have been invested in arms, were expended in sending numbers of useless "officers" from this country. . . . We only wish it to be understood that we are not in favour of consuming money in sending over considerable bodies of men from this side, unless in an expedition, until everything is ready to begin the work, and the torch prepared to ignite the pile.[1]

It is difficult to judge these men. In many ways they were realists, tough-minded and even ruthless in dealing with each other, enormously attentive to the details of their conspiracies, and dedicated to the point of bankrupting themselves. Yet about their efforts there is that atmosphere of unreality which dominated the Fenians. The Clansmen conducted their affairs as though they represented a great power. They were overwhelmed perhaps by the realization of the enormous numbers of Irish dispersed throughout the world (originally, the seventh seat on the revolutionary directory was reserved for a representative of the down-under Irish in Australia and New Zealand) and were convinced that somehow a formula could be hit upon that would unite them all. Hope and frustration alternate in their correspondence, and inevitably bitterness and recrimination followed upon even successful projects.

The Clan had in the 1870's one great success—a success that suggests the kind of work for which the organization was best fitted. Six Fenians were still confined to the British penal colony of Western Australia, and it was a point of honor with the men released in 1870 to rescue their comrades. A whaling ship, the *Catalpa*, was purchased and outfitted in New Bedford for a year's cruise to the whaling grounds of the South Atlantic and South Pacific. In March, 1876, it put into Bunbury, Australia. There, contact was made with Clan agents, and the prisoners taken off. Thirty thousand dollars was raised for the expedition and, significantly, though a good many persons were informed (including Senator S. B. Conover, who offered the aid of a revenue cutter), the secret was well kept until the ship was homeward bound. It deposited its escapees in New York on August 19, and then proceeded to New Bedford, where booming cannon welcomed it, and John Boyle O'Reilly made the reception speech.

While Devoy was making his way within the Clan na Gael, O'Donovan Rossa in 1877 became the Head Center of the Fenian Brotherhood, or what remained of it. But, more important, he also became the director of a fund to carry on guerrilla warfare against the British Empire.

The Skirmishing Fund, as it was called, was established in response to an anonymous letter, which appeared in the *Irish World*, September 4, 1875. The letter called for militant action, which "does more to keep the faith alive than a thousand sensible, prudent, wiseheaded patriots who crawl on crutches . . . into forgotten graves." The *Irish World* editor responded enthusiastically. There were sufficient Irish in England, it asserted, to "give London to flames and reduce Liverpool to disaster . . . spread through all the emporia of England, terror, conflagration, and irretrievable destruction." After further meditation, the paper on December 4, declared that there were at least thirty million people throughout the entire world tied to Ireland by blood or sympathy. They lacked only leadership. "The Irish cause requires skirmishers. It requires a little band of heroes who will initiate and keep up without intermission a guerrilla war. . . ."[2] Rossa responded to the call. In a letter of December 5 requesting use of the *Irish World* to raise the necessary money, Rossa proposed action to free those Fenians still in British prisons. He was frank about his plans. If in a foray skirmishers were captured and sentenced to execution, "I would feel warranted in hanging the ministers that ordered the murder, or in burning the town or city they were to be hanged in. . . ."[3] Ford hesitated for three months before publishing Rossa's letter and turning over the responsibility to him, perhaps because of the rumors circulating among

Rossa's friends that his mind had been affected by imprisonment. The *Irish World* editor also took the precaution of appointing one of his own staff to act as fund treasurer.

To judge from the letters that accompanied many subscriptions, the contributors were often the most frenetic of Irishmen. Their shrillness brings us deep into the tensions of the depression years. A John McEntee of Florence, South Carolina, sent his pittance "to purchase poison stilettoes and lucifer matches." A "Railroad Man" from Texas, upon reading of Rossa's plan to saturate the House of Commons with osmic gas, felt his heart jump with joy. "Twenty years of knocking around has hardened my heart, so that I would like to see bottled death used in a manner that all the English enemy could be enclosed in the bottle after the osmium got out." Some $23,000 was collected in the first year, with 30,000 contributors sending money from England, Scotland, Canada, Ireland, and, of course, the United States. Though the Skirmishing Fund was condemned from many an altar, some contributors were Catholic priests, and the *Western Watchman* of St. Louis, edited by the unruly Father David Phelan, endorsed the enterprise.

Time soon demonstrated that Rossa was a highly frivolous administrator. His conduct lacked even that measure of decorum demanded by those who sympathized with his bloodthirsty projects. He made of the Skirmishing Fund page in the *Irish World* a kind of Irish gossip column. Old friends were genially greeted and told the news, such as when Rossa last saw "Ned Duffy, who's now dead, at Ballaghadereen," and that "Paddy Lennon, who took part in the Dublin Risings, is in Albany now." He blackmailed others who did not contribute by publicly declaring them traitors to Ireland. And all the while he indulged conspicuously in dramatic self-pity. "It was under Gladstone's regime that I could not get a spoon to eat my pint of stirabout, and with my hands tied, had to go at it with knees and elbows on the ground in a black hole."

Neither Rossa nor his followers defended terrorism in terms of the anarchist theories then rapidly winning adherents in Europe and the United States. They had inherited their hatreds and were prepared to discuss them historically, but saw little need for more abstract speculation. For the truth was simple and obvious: skirmishers were engaged in no less than a holy war to avenge the dead. Blood cried out for it, and no holds were barred. To have scruples about the choice of weapons was to permit England the right of defining the terms of war. From this point of view, skirmishing was little more than Whiteboyism, that nightmare of earlier nationalists. The following letter from a B. K. Kennedy, Black Hank, Colorado, June 7, 1877, to Rossa makes the point. The subject of the letter's proposal was the Earl of Leitrim, destined to be murdered in the following year.

> I take the liberty of writing to you on a subject nearest my heart, that is, to do my Native land some good. I was born in the County of Leitrim close to the Lord's mansion and I am acquainted a little around there. Now what I want to say is this, would you want a little skirmishing done around there? I have a crow to pick with his Lordship. . . . Now regarding myself, I am twenty-one years of age, got a good common school education and I flatter myself as being pretty smart. You will say his writing don't show it; don't trouble about that. . . . I belonged to the Leitrim militia and army reserve at one time, got into trouble one twelfth of July [the day on which Orangemen parade in commemoration of King William's victory over James II in the Battle of the Boyne], had to skin out in a hurry. . . . Tell me if you can actually give me anything to do. If not, I was thinking of doing a little on my own hook.[4]

The gentleman's code of honor, which had ennobled Young Ireland, clearly had no place in the Skirmishing Fund. Nationalism had gone down a long and dangerous road since Davis' time. John O'Leary, who deplored the Skirmishers and later the dynamiters, expressed cogently the older faith when he told the poet, William Butler Yeats, "There are some things a man must not do for his country." And yet hadn't the Young Irelanders been more than a little ridiculous? And wasn't O'Leary's life after 1865 a long paralysis?

The skirmishers reflected the growing violence of the American working classes in the last years of the 1870's, as police brutality in suppressing street demonstrations and strikes forced the workers to arm themselves. They reflected also in their Irish way that growing mood of desperation which overcame the European rebel in the last half of the nineteenth century, as decades of disillusionment made him despair of ever winning the Rights of Man. In Ireland, Italy, Germany, and Russia the rebel was marked by a sense of absolute virtue, absolutely frustrated. Alfred Nobel's invention of dynamite in 1866 excited him by its promise. In the following decades monarchs and other men of power walked in fear and danger. The International Working People's Association, in which a frequent contributor to the *Irish World*, Dyer D. Lum, was active, led the way in domesticating European theories of anarchy in the United States.

The terrorists were lonely men, gifted and anxious for power, yet powerless. For them terrorism was to act, and to act was power. "I am now five years out of prison, and have done nothing but belong to two revolutionary societies," wrote Rossa in undertaking the skirmishing assignment. ". . . The work is too slow, and the time flies too fast to feed my hope of doing something or seeing something done before I die." And terrorism for these strangely afflicted men was also an intoxication. Patrick J. P. Tynan, one of the Invincibles who in Dublin's Phoenix Park in 1882 murdered Lord Frederick Cavendish, Chief Secretary for Ireland, and Thomas Burke, the Undersecretary, described the crime's effect upon one of the assassins in these words:

> K—— was in a reverie as the incident was closing, when he was aroused by the action of one of the sacred band nearby. He became conscious; he was the possessor of a fierce, strange joy; an emotion never to be forgotten pervaded his whole being. Not one man belonging to that sacred band had the smallest personal feeling toward the slain foe. Their souls were filled with the

purity and patriotism of their acts. They recognized the important truth that they were humble instruments in the hands of Providence, to punish in some measure the many sacrilegious crimes committed by the arrogant invaders on their bleeding country.[5]

The Skirmishing Fund in its early years, despite Rossa's bravado, was drawn upon chiefly to subsidize propaganda rather than terrorism. Money from the fund was used to ship the body of John O'Mahony, a founding father of Fenianism who died in 1877, back to Ireland for burial. In accordance with the ironic Irish practice, those who castigated him in life tendered him a magnificent funeral. The purpose, of course, as Dr. Carroll said, was to stir up the "dry bones at home." Carroll himself drew from the fund to pay the expenses of a trip to Ireland, and the *Irish World* tapped it to get over a financial crisis in 1879. However useful these expenditures, they were hardly the objects for which the money was collected and gave color to the charges of abuse of trust that the fund seemed spontaneously to generate.

The Skirmishing Fund represented the single largest nationalist treasury in the United States, and inevitably it aroused concern within the Clan na Gael, whose leaders feared the influence it gave to Patrick Ford and his social theories. By 1877, however, when the fund had acquired about $48,000, control had passed entirely into the hands of trustees who were Clan na Gael men. Rossa's embarrassing shenanigans may have persuaded Ford that it was not wise to be responsible for the money, or it may have been that his increasing dedication to social reform altered his views on Ireland's need for guerrilla warfare. Whatever the reason, the Clan na Gael won control and thus strengthened its position. It was now clearly the most powerful and respected body of revolutionary nationalists on either side of the Atlantic.

The Clan, however, was not by any means the largest Irish-American organization. The Irish Catholic Benevolent Union, for example, had a membership nearly twice as large and a far fatter treasury. Secrecy cut the Clan off from popular support and kept it under clerical fire. Nor could the Clan claim to express adequately the aspirations of Irish-America. "We have in this country Fenians, nationalists, Home Rulers, and Repealers," wrote Dillon O'Brien, ardent leader of the Minnesota Catholic Colonization movement in 1877. "All are good true men, but all are more or less like jealous peddlers, praising their own wares and decrying the wares of others."[6] O'Brien proposed that a national convention be called which would be truly representative of all the factions and interests of Irish-America.

The proposal was widely endorsed. Irish-America longed for solidarity but was incapable of achieving it unaided. The immigrant community too closely reflected the divisions of class and section within American life, and personal and organizational jealousies were too intense. Nationalism, the consciousness of being Irish and downtrodden, alone provided a basis for collective action. A quickening of that consciousness was imperative to cut through the animosities that divided Irish-Americans. That could only come from a revival of militant nationalism in Ireland.

The resurgence of nationalism in Ireland in the 1870's occurred under the unusual auspices of Irish conservatives. In 1869 the English Liberal party, led by William Ewart Gladstone, had persuaded Parliament to disestablish the Church of Ireland—the church of the Ascendancy—and in the following year to enact the first important Irish land reform legislation.

By these measures English liberalism frightened Irish conservatism. Of what benefit, reasoned some influential members of the Ascendancy, is a union with England which places the privileged peoples of Ireland at the mercy of the recently enfranchised English democracy. Foremost among those who took up this line of thought was Isaac Butt. A magnificent Dublin personality and a responsible conservative, he wanted the traditional leaders of Irish society to avert disaster by putting their house in order. Catholics, he thought, would support Ascendancy leadership if their just grievances were removed. In 1874 he founded the Irish Home Rule party.

By Home Rule he meant a federal arrangement between Britain and Ireland, whereby the latter would have its own legislature to govern purely Irish affairs, leaving foreign affairs and other matters to the Westminster Parliament. Butt entered the parliamentary session of 1874 with 59 followers more or less committed to Home Rule, the largest nationalist party since O'Connell's time. Within two years the party had demonstrated its incompetence to achieve its objective, and Butt was under heavy criticism.

The party's failure, like that of the independent Irish party in the 1850's, resulted from its inability to control the selection and nomination of its members. In this process landlord and clerical influence was paramount. Without this power Butt could not ensure control over his party in the House of Commons. As a consequence, government job-seekers, only nominally interested in Home Rule, were too plentiful in the party. His basic political strategy also imposed difficulties. The party was shaped by conservative concern not to injure Ascendancy interests and feelings, but many of its members represented Catholic, and some even Fenian, interests. Without good luck and strong leadership, a group that included Colonel King Harman, an Ascendancy magnifico, and Joseph Biggar, a wealthy Belfast provision merchant and member of the Irish Republic Brotherhood (I.R.B.), could not look forward to much except trouble.[7]

By 1877 the party's inadequacies had cost it important Fenian support in Britain. Butt had earlier won the hearts of Fenians when, at great financial sacrifice, he had defended them in court and later took a leading part in the Amnesty movement to secure their freedom. Their affection was of no inconsiderable political importance. Their organized Tammany tactics made them formidable opponents. In Ireland they were hostile to Home Rule, but out of regard for Butt they refrained for a time from bullying his party. In England and Scotland the Home Rule movement rested squarely on the Home Rule Confederation in which North of England Fenians played leading roles.

The Irish in England were if anything more fiercely nationalistic than the American Irish. Residence in the Lancashire ghettos had rendered them intensely aware of Ireland and of themselves as Irish. They were, in the opinion of John Devoy, almost a caste apart. The pressures upon them were probably greater than those upon the American Irish. As late as 1872, the Irish in the Black Country of the North had to fight for their lives and their churches against No Popery mobs. John Barry, born in County Wexford but raised in the North of England, a witty businessman and member of the I.R.B. supreme council, was the chief organizer of the Irish in England, Wales, and Scotland. In January, 1873, he formed a confederation of the Home Rule clubs already in existence and persuaded Butt to accept the presidency. The Home Rule Confederation mattered because the Reform Act of 1867, which extended the franchise to the working classes of England, made the Irish navvy's vote of consequence in British politics.

As Butt's leadership faltered, a number of younger members of his party caught the imagination of the discontented Fenians. Known to Irish history as obstructionists or activists, these men of the future were engaged in filibustering in the House of Commons. Rather than conciliate the House, as Butt tried to do, they set it by its ears with a tireless stream of talk and other obstructive tactics designed to focus attention upon Irish affairs and to persuade the English that both peoples would be better off were the Irish to have their own legislature in which to talk. Joseph Biggar, the ungainly Belfast merchant, was perhaps the first exponent of the practice. When an Irish coercion bill was under debate in April, 1875, he rose to speak at five o'clock and, to the disgust of the House, did not sit down again until nine. He filled the intervening hours by reading hesitantly and almost inaudibly from parliamentary blue books. The majority of his associates thought this most unseemly behavior. "I think," said one, "that a man should be a gentleman first and a patriot afterwards."

Among those not inclined to condemn Biggar's tactics was Charles Stewart Parnell, a gentleman undeniably, who first took his seat in the House on the very day of Biggar's speech. The descendant of an old County Wicklow Ascendancy family, and as such cordially welcomed by the party's conservative wing, Parnell would within the year join Biggar in the despised practice of obstruction. To the English press Biggar was comic and grotesque. "Mr. Biggar brings the manner of his store into this illustrious assembly," said the *World* of London, "and his manner even for a Belfast store is very bad. When he rises to address the House, as he did at least ten times last night . . . the air is heavy with the odor of kippered herring." But Parnell, with his cold and aristocratic bearing, was not easily ridiculed. After an uncertain beginning, he soon proved a formidable parliamentary tactician. In the session of 1877, Parnell and a handful of others forced the House on one occasion to sit continuously from four in the afternoon until after six the next evening. This record endured until 1881, when the Irish, tenaciously fighting a coercion bill, made the House sit for forty-two hours, whereupon tradition was broken and cloture invoked to end the debate.

Parnell was both a glory and a puzzle to his contemporaries. He remains a puzzle to historians. Why did he break with his class and lead a social and political revolution that shook the Cromwellian settlement to its foundation? Perhaps he was influenced by his mother. She was a daughter of Commodore Stewart, commander of "Old Ironsides" in the War of 1812, and a highly neurotic Anglophobe. Perhaps it was a visit to America in 1871 that transformed this then rather conventional landlord into a nationalist. While in the United States, he suffered the indignity of being identified with the poor and despised immigrant. He reacted by defending the Irish character and so made an important commitment. On that trip he also learned something about Irish possibilities. The spectacle of former peasants elevated to the ranks of businessmen and politicians convinced him, as it did many others, that "if Irishmen were self-reliant and stuck to each other, they could make themselves felt everywhere."[8]

The formation of Parnell's character owed much to England, where he received what little formal education he possessed. Many of his closest Irish associates thought him essentially English, and he in turn looked upon these somewhat raw and aspiring men with an English aristocrat's contempt. As a politician he was cool and detached, but he was at the same time superstitious and given to eccentricity in dress and behavior. As John Boyle O'Reilly pointed out upon first meeting him, he knew when to talk and when not to talk. And he could be very silent. He displayed publicly none of the sentiment that convention ascribes to the Irish. Even on the occasion of what was perhaps his greatest personal triumph, when the House of Commons rose to its feet to cheer him, he gave no outward sign that he was moved or even interested. He was withal a very lonely man, and this proved to be his undoing.

Whatever the sources of Parnell's detachment, it gave him profound advantages in the competition for leadership over the Irish people. His courage and political intelligence though great were perhaps no greater than others', but he employed them ruthlessly, concerned only for the political realities and indifferent to the sacred atmosphere of the Mother of Parliaments which so overawed Butt and most other Irishmen.

Parnell's detachment also freed him from the class concerns of the Irish conservatives. The emergent English democracy, so troubling to Butt, offered Parnell opportunities to bring his name forward, and he did not hesitate to take advantage of them. Along with John O'Connor Power and Frank Hugh O'Donnell, two other young Irish obstructionists, Parnell appeared frequently before working-class audiences to support radical reforms and to expound the line that English radicalism was the ally of Irish nationalism. Though the events of the 1880's would not bear out this proposition, it appeared to have some basis in fact in the late 1870's. "The interests of the English and Irish people are identical," declared George Mitchell of the British Agricultural Laborers Union. "We both want perfect self-government, and whether we govern jointly or severally is for each nation to decide by popular vote."[9]

Parnell's driving ambition also led him to solicit the aid of the

Fenians in Britain, without whose support he could not hope to wrest power from Butt. With the help of John Barry, who organized a series of meetings for him in the summer of 1877, he won over the Fenians; and in August, 1877, he was elected to replace Butt as head of the British Home Rule Confederation.

The grandson of Commodore Stewart now had behind him the most formidable Irish organization in Britain. But he still lacked sufficient strength in Ireland, where the conservative Home Rulers maintained their grip. At the national conference of Home Rule organizations in Ireland, held in Dublin in the middle of January, 1878, he successfully packed the meeting with his supporters from across the Irish Sea, but he refused to make a direct bid for leadership. He was young, he said, and could wait.

Both O'Donnell and Power were also young and also very ambitious. They, too, wanted to lead. They suffered, however, from certain limitations: Power, for all his brilliance, was too much an opportunist, and O'Donnell possessed a conceit bordering on megalomania. Moreover, it is doubtful that a people accustomed to the rule of their betters, to whom Sadleir and Keogh had revealed the moral deficiencies of the new *bourgeoisie*, would submit to the leadership of an O'Connor Power or an O'Donnell. As a landlord and a Protestant, Parnell was a personage whom the Irish had been trained to respect, if not love (before his death he, or the myth he became, would have their love too). O'Donnell records a conversation he had with the rugged Galway Fenian, Mat Harris, who explained his preference for Parnell:

> We are a nation of Catholics and we want a Protestant. It looks well. We are a nation of peasants and we want a landlord to head us. It looks well. You are neither a Protestant nor a landlord. Parnell is both.[10]

Parnell's star was in the ascendancy, but its path was yet uncertain, and there were many obstacles to overcome.

There was above all the necessity of winning support from the Clan na Gael revolutionaries in the United States. By 1877, as already mentioned, they had established good working relations with the I.R.B., gained control over the Skirmishing Fund, and vigorously demonstrated the Clan's superiority to the Fenian Brotherhood. The rise of Parnell and the work of the obstructionists presented the American revolutionaries with difficulties. Orthodoxy taught them that to participate in Irish politics was in effect to recognize the legitimacy of British rule in Ireland—recognition that was at odds with their oath of loyalty to the shadowy Irish Republic of their dreams. Moreover, they were convinced that nothing but trouble could come from nationalist participation in parliamentary politics; on this point the history of the parliamentary movement of the 1840's and 1850's appeared conclusive. The American extremists were especially angry with O'Connor Power who held a seat in Parliament while serving on the I.R.B. supreme council. Power had come to New York in 1875 to speak at Cooper Union in support of Irish land reform and Butt's federalism, which he likened to American constitutional arrangements between federal and state governments. The Cooper Union speeches constituted a prologue to the New Departure, which will be discussed in the next chapter, calling as they did for the open participation by nationalists of all persuasions in the work of the Home Rule party. In 1875, however, Power only made enemies among the doctrinaire nationalists. In August, 1877, he was expelled from the I.R.B. council along with Joseph Biggar; at the same time John Barry, the Lancashire organizer of the Home Rule Confederation of Great Britain, and Patrick Egan, who will later figure in these pages, were forced to resign. The break with Power, which took place in the same month that Parnell was elected president of the Home Rule Confederation, cost the I.R.B. dearly. Power had a strong following among Fenians in the North of England and in Ireland, many of whom thereafter broke with the supreme council when he was expelled.

Parnell was, of course, exempt from this kind of bigotry. He had demonstrated a degree of nationalist enthusiasm far beyond that expected of a landlord, and he was in no way bound by Fenian dogma. He had first attracted Irish-American attention when in 1876, on the occasion of the centennial celebration of American independence, he journeyed to Washington in the company of O'Connor Power to present President Grant with a message of congratulation from the Irish people. (Grant refused to accept the message, which would have violated protocol and embarrassed the British Embassy. The House of Representatives, however, was receptive.) It was in the following year of 1877 that the physical force men, as they liked to call themselves, first took Parnell's measure. James J. O'Kelly met him in Paris and reported to Devoy in a letter of August 5, 1877, that he was "cool— extremely so and resolute." O'Kelly was a good judge of such qualities, having, among other adventures, served with the French Foreign Legion before coming to New York in 1871, where he, too, found a place on Bennett's *Herald* and would in time become its drama critic. In his Paris letter he urged that the Clan throw its support to the young aristocrat. But at this stage of the game Devoy and Carroll were anxious to make Parnell one of their own rather than back him in what they considered to be the folly of constitutional agitation.

The events of the following six months would alter Clan na Gael attitudes as the revolutionaries ran into a sea of troubles. The defection of members following upon O'Connor Power's expulsion in August, 1877, was shortly followed by a challenge from James Stephens, the old Fenian chief, who came forward after the death of O'Mahoney to reassert his former leadership. His name retained just enough of its old glamour to win him important support from I.R.B. men in the Irish counties of Dublin, Louth, and Wexford, and among many New York and Boston Irish. Devoy and Carroll were merciless in attacking him. In the fall and winter of 1877, the work of the revolutionaries was all but stopped by the bitter feuds which set Irishmen at each others' throats. To add to Clan na Gael troubles, O'Donovan Rossa's drunkenness and public shenanigans were threatening the life of the Skirmishing Fund.

Dr. Carroll, therefore, was not very hopeful when, subsidized by Skirmishing Fund money, he sailed for Europe in late November or early December, 1877. He joined O'Kelly in Madrid and together they unsuccessfully presented to the Spanish government a plan for seizing Gibraltar. The inevitable rebuff, added to O'Kelly's arguments, probably persuaded Carroll to think better of the Home Rule party and constitutional agitation along the lines followed by the obstructionists. In January, 1878, the Doctor met Parnell in London and, as he wrote many years later, was pleased with the younger man's cautious statement that he was in favor of absolute independence for Ireland. Parnell furthered assured him that "when the people so declared he would go with them." Carroll in turn assured Parnell that "we would be his friends and would ask our friends there to support him in all that he did toward that end."[11] The friends Carroll alluded to were the members of the I.R.B. supreme council. They were not to be won over.

In the middle of March, 1878, Parnell accompanied by Frank Hugh O'Donnell and another obstructionist met with Carroll and his friends, the fastidious John O'Leary and the irascible John O'Connor, in Carroll's London hotel. James J. O'Kelly was present as a friend of both parties. In that hotel room, O'Leary and O'Connor faced the revolutionary's classic dilemma. They could abstain from public life and its corruptions, nourishing their honor and feeding their souls on a vision of the ultimate revolutionary drama; or they could join the politicians in seeking beneficial legislation from a government whose legitimacy they denied. In the first course there was the danger of losing touch with the people and indeed all reality; in the second, of losing in the busy workaday world that shimmering ideal of freedom that made their loneliness bearable.

According to O'Donnell's account, O'Leary opened the meeting by revealing his disdain for the filibusterers. Irish freedom, he said, could not be obtained by keeping the British Prime Minister out of bed until dawn. Parnell with his gift for silence was impressively reserved. The shadow of O'Connor Power, according to Devoy's account, fell across the meeting. The I.R.B. men were fearful that any connection with constitutional action would dishonor them as they believed it had him. No one could persuade them otherwise. They chose to follow the first course. What is of the greatest significance is that the discussion revolved around the question of aiding Parnell. Gone, apparently, was the hope of getting him to subordinate his newly won authority to the interests of the revolutionaries.[12]

By 1878, when the five-year-old depression in the United States was dragging to a close, the pattern that the crisis of the 1880's would follow was already emerging. Parnell's leadership was widely, if not always graciously, recognized. The I.R.B. chieftains were hostile, but the American revolutionaries were moving toward Parnell. The deep-felt desire, made urgent by the hard times, for a new nationalist movement that would raise up the Irish everywhere was close to being fulfilled. But the rumblings of social revolution were also beginning to be heard. Great Britain was still struggling with bad times. Under the pressure of American grain competition, prices for British and Irish foodstuffs were falling, and wet summers in 1877 and 1878 made for a critical shortage of potatoes in the West of Ireland. A peasant revolt was beginning to flicker in County Mayo. The search for social justice which the depression had stimulated in the United States had made of the land question an obsession for many. Both the social and the nationalist movement aimed at regeneration of the Irish; both drew sympathetic support from the same people, and had the land question as a common denominator; both movements encouraged violence among those for whom frustration was an agony. Yet in the 1880's the two would clash head on. The signs of future trouble were apparent in the skepticism expressed by the *Irish World* on October 5, 1878: "Where does Mr. Parnell propose to lead us? To the hills and pastures of Ireland, or into the division lobbies of the 'grand old English Parliament'?"

I have worked at breaking stone when the cold was such that the birds would drop dead around me, and was unconscious of it, so intently was I thinking out the true solution of Ireland's difficulties. When I came out I was armed with a plan of which the Land League is the result.

MICHAEL DAVITT on the New Departure,
Boston *Pilot*, July 8, 1882

We know from their own lips that it was their purpose to use every wheel and lever of the organization under their guidance to celebrate the centennial of 1782 by a unanimous demand for the government of Ireland by the Irish.

JOHN BOYLE O'REILLY on the New Departure,
Boston *Pilot*, December 17, 1881

CHAPTER FIVE

The New Departure

I N the New Departure, whose origins this chapter will discuss, the grand coalition for which Irishmen had so long been groping was finally consummated. Fenian and parliamentarian, peasant-terrorist and priest, exile and stay-at-home were brought together under Parnell's leadership to shake the United Kingdom to its foundations. In the opinion of one British historian, the New Departure was "nothing less than the strongest native revolt for over two hundred years."[1]

The coalition broke Anglo-Irish control over the land and laid the groundwork for the modern nation of peasant proprietors. The Irish Question was made the first order of business in British politics, and the English Liberal party was converted to the cause of Irish self-government. The towering figure in all of this was Parnell. By shaping the forces of the coalition according to his own vision he ruled Ireland in the 1880's as an "uncrowned king."

There is a traditional story of the New Departure's origins that has all the qualities of an epic. Michael Davitt is the hero, and the legend owes something to his sponsorship. According to this account, Davitt spent the long years in Dartmoor prison, after being sentenced in 1870, mulling over possible ways to unite the Irish people behind the nationalist cause. Released in December,

1877, he shortly afterward came to the United States to persuade Irish-Americans to accept the plan he had hit upon. The plan closely resembled that which Fintan Lalor had urged upon Young Ireland in 1847–48: the national movement was to be linked to the engine of agrarian unrest. As embodied in the Land League in 1879, the scheme was sufficiently practical to enlist the hitherto anti-nationalist tenant farmers and sufficiently militant to hold the Fenian rank and file. Moreover, it was a constitutional movement that the Irish Home Rule party could advocate in the House of Commons. Davitt, therefore, according to this tradition, brilliantly solved the problem that had so long troubled nationalists, and in doing so profoundly influenced the course of modern Irish history.

The trouble with this story is that it credits Davitt with a prescience that he did not possess, confuses the Land League with the New Departure, and misinterprets the nature of both. The true story is more complex and less dramatic.

The Land League had its origins in the near-famine that afflicted Ireland in 1879; the New Departure, in the yearning of Irishmen everywhere, but especially in the United States, for a new political movement that would unite them and confound their enemies. As originally conceived, the New Departure looked forward to a political revolution. Its authors hoped to celebrate the victory won by the Irish Volunteers in 1782, when they coerced England to grant Ireland an independent parliament, with a similar victory in 1882.

When Michael Davitt was released from prison in 1877, nationalists, whether of the constitutional or the revolutionary variety, were anxious for change. But they were uncertain as to the direction they should take. The centennial of 1782 was approaching, and they looked to it as the year of deliverance. They were encouraged by the prospect that Anglo-Russian tensions would bring John Bull into war with the Russian bear and so provide them with the opportunities that the American Revolution had given Grattan. After the Berlin Congress of 1878, which eased the critical Balkan situation, nationalists pinned their hopes on British troubles in Afghanistan; still later in 1879, they were forced to look for opportunities in the struggles the Zulus were waging against the British in South Africa.

In June, 1878, two months before Davitt arrived in the United States, John Boyle O'Reilly suggested a course of action, should an Anglo-Russian war come. A national convention should be called, wrote the *Pilot* editor, representative of all the corporate bodies in the country, public and private, and of all shades of Irish opinion. The convention should demand restoration of the 1782 Parliament. If granted, then "away with disunion and disloyalty; if not, let Ireland prepare for war."[2]

Another intriguing possibility was suggested by the filibustering practices of Parnell and his associates in the House of Commons. These infuriated the overwhelming majority of House members, making it probable that sooner or later the offensive Irish members would be suspended and ejected. If such a crisis should occur, reasoned a number of theorists, the Home Rulers could then formally secede from Parliament and set themselves up in Dublin as Ireland's provisional government. Parnell in May, 1878, at St. Helens, Lancashire, held out such a prospect to an enthusiastic audience of Lancashire Irishmen.[3]

The difficulty with these various proposals was that Irish public opinion in Ireland was hardly prepared for them. Parnell's filibustering band numbered no more than six or seven, and he did not yet have control of the Home Rule party. O'Reilly in Boston could talk about a national convention, but the Irish people at home would not support such a resolute course of action. The revolutionaries knew this and were troubled by it. They were fast realizing that, if they were to shape Irish public opinion, it would be necessary for them to abandon their traditional scruples against participating in movements of purely social or political reform. O'Connor Power, the Fenian who had taken a seat in

Parliament, was reviled for his apostasy, but the path he followed possessed attractive possibilities.

The Ballot Act of 1872, which provided for the secret ballot, promised to open up Irish politics by protecting the tenant farmer's vote from the scrutiny of landlord and priest. Also promising was the movement to extend the franchise so as to include agricultural laborers. Land and educational reforms were among the popular causes to which the nationalists might commit themselves in the hope of winning greater public favor. The approach of the 1782 centenary rendered urgent the need to infuse the Irish mind with a heightened sense of nationalism.

Davitt had learned about Parnell's work while in Dartmoor. Shortly after his release he was introduced to the young aristocrat. Parnell was impressed by Davitt, as was Dr. Carroll, then engaged in exploring the situation in Ireland. In the spring of 1878, Davitt made a speaking tour through the North of England and Scotland during which he pleaded for mutual tolerance among Irishmen of different political viewpoints. Richard Pigott, later notorious as the forger of letters damaging to Parnell, criticized these talks for their apparent abandonment of intransigent Fenianism. In answering, Davitt declared that he kept to the old faith, that he desired no connection with constitutional agitation or parliamentary parties. His aim, he said, was simply to smother internecine animosities.

Davitt had rejoined the I.R.B. shortly after leaving prison and had taken a seat on the supreme council as representative for the North of England. The answer to Pigott, written two months before he sailed to the United States, suggests that Davitt differed from his die-hard associates on the council only in that he had a broader understanding of the nationalists' historic function to unify the Irish people. Nevertheless, there is no reason to doubt that Davitt shared in the desire to strike out in new directions characteristic at this time of so many thoughtful nationalists. The legendary assertion, however, that he emerged from prison "with the Land League in his brain" is not supported by his actions in 1878 in either the Old World or the New.

Davitt came to the United States chiefly to visit his mother, who lived in New Jersey. He was persuaded to prolong his stay by Devoy and Carroll, who promised him a lecture tour that would leave him richer than he was when he arrived. Whatever convictions he held on the need for change, he was caution itself in his early appearances on lecture platforms in New York and Philadelphia. His first important statement, definitely foreshadowing the New Departure, was given in Brooklyn's New Park Theater on October 13, 1878. We may be sure that it was the fruit of many midnight deliberations among Davitt, Devoy, and Carroll.

He opened by calling the Home Rule movement organized hypocrisy, much as Devoy, Ford, and others had done earlier. Very likely these remarks were designed to dispel any notions of a weakening of Fenian fervor by the proposals that followed. He then urged nationalists to support political and social reforms and nationalist candidates for Parliament substantially as Parnell had in his St. Helens speech in the spring. Because the secret ballot had rendered the peasant politically independent, the time was ripe, said Davitt, to nationalize politics. Every elective office from Member of Parliament to Poor Law Guardian must be filled with believers in Irish independence. Thus the spirit of nationalism would be infused everywhere, "in the representative assembly as well as in the individual's breast, be it under the peasant's cloak or the robe of the clergyman."

Considerable confusion attended Davitt's talk. According to an account written by Devoy in 1906, Davitt's speech as originally prepared called for a solution of Ireland's land question along the lines of the famous "Three F's": fair rents fixed by impartial evaluation, fixity of tenure as long as rents were paid, and free sale of improvements made to holdings. These proposals were first championed by the independent Irish party in the 1850's and later by Isaac Butt. They were hopelessly outdated in the view of

Devoy and others, who persuaded Davitt to change them. Through a mistake not uncommon to lecturers, Davitt brought the original manuscript to Brooklyn and then was so flustered that he made a poor speech. The dissatisfied audience thereupon called for Devoy. As he came forward he noticed the entire Ford family sitting in the front row. "There was a cloud on Patrick Ford's face that presaged a coming storm." To appease the *Irish World* editor, Devoy spoke more radically on the land question than he otherwise would have.

He first drew upon his own humiliating experience when in 1876 he had attempted to interest the Russian ambassador in an alliance with Irish republicans. It was a persuasive approach. Should an Anglo-Russian war break out, he said, it would be the duty of nationalists to approach Russia again. They could expect a cold answer: "Gentlemen, we have no doubt of your sincerity but you are only a small party; you don't represent Ireland. . . . All your members of Parliament are loyal to England. . . ." If nationalists entered public life, however, all would be changed. Public opinion would be reshaped, authentic nationalists would represent the nation, and the way would be prepared for revolution whenever Russia or any other enemy of England offered the opportunity.

Devoy then addressed himself to the land question in a way more calculated to please Patrick Ford than Davitt had employed.

> I think the only true solution of the land question is the abolition of landlordism. . . . The land of Ireland belongs to the people of Ireland. . . . I believe in Irish independence, but I don't think it would be worthwhile to free Ireland if that foreign landlord system were left standing.

With Ford presumably appeased, Devoy then proceeded to advocate the solution earlier agreed upon. Destruction of landlordism could not be achieved in a day, he said, "therefore I think we should . . . accept all measures looking to the prevention of arbitrary evictions and the creation of a peasant proprietary as a step in the right direction."[4]

Devoy had good reason to be anxious about Ford's good will, for his paper's grip on the immigrant working classes was very strong. Davitt's meetings were only lightly attended, and he needed sympathetic publicity. According to Devoy, Ford later admitted that had it not been for Devoy's speech that evening, he would have felt it necessary to denounce Davitt and the meeting.[5] Even so, the *Irish World* gave only scant attention to the doings of Davitt and Devoy. Truncated versions of Davitt's talks were relegated to the paper's back pages. The Greenback campaign of 1878 and the demagoguery of Denis Kearney and Ben Butler got much more attention.

Ford's disinterest was no doubt due to the fact that land reform, the *Irish World's* magnificent obsession, was then only of secondary interest to Davitt and Devoy. Letters in *Devoy's Post Bag* written in this period reveal that they were concerned with many things—with the strengthening of the Clan na Gael and the I.R.B., with the prospects of founding a newspaper in Dublin, with the possibilities of English involvement in war, but *not* with land reform in Ireland. Ford eventually gave his approval to the New Departure, though not enthusiastically and only because he was assured the Home Rulers planned to withdraw from Parliament—a move he hoped would stimulate discussion of the land question.[6]

Misunderstanding launched the New Departure. In October, 1878, the Home Rule Confederation of Great Britain held a conference, against the wishes of Isaac Butt, and re-elected Parnell as president. Devoy, misinformed, assumed that Parnell had at last broken with the conservative Irish leader. After consultation with other Clan members, but not with Davitt, then in the Midwest, Devoy made the decision to commit the nationalists to Parnell on certain conditions. A telegram was dispatched to the Irish leader assuring him of support if, among other things, he would agree to the following:

(1) Substitution of a general declaration in favor of Irish self-government for the federalist plan of home rule.

(2) Vigorous agitation to achieve peasant proprietorship as the ultimate solution of the land question, and acceptance of any concessions that would in the meantime increase tenant security.

On October 26, 1878, the day following dispatch of the telegram, Devoy had it printed in the New York *Herald,* along with a series of rigged "interviews" with leading nationalists. In this piece of public relations work, the term "New Departure" was used for the first time and its essential meaning made clear. The heirs of Wolfe Tone were leaving the underground only that they might do a better job of schooling the Irish people in nationalism. Land, educational, and local government reforms were to be taken up, but only as a means toward the nationalizing of Irish public opinion. It was not expected that the British government would confer many favors. Self-government, the grand prize, would have to be won by physical force or the threat of physical force. When popular enthusiasm was sufficiently strong, or war or revolution had weakened England, "we can command our representatives to withdraw from the British Parliament and meet in Ireland as an Irish legislature." This gloss on the October 26 telegram makes it clear enough that the authors were not sponsoring a peasant uprising but a political revolution.

The New Departure had one of its most enthusiastic supporters in John Boyle O'Reilly. It was fully in accord with the spirit of his own proposal earlier. At first he was under the false impression that Davitt and Devoy were proposing more or less immediate action. On November 2, the *Pilot* announced that the Parnellites "are to demand home rule and cooperate in blocking the House of Commons until the demand is granted or they are expelled." He was no less enthusiastic after it was explained to him in Boston in December that the revolutionaries were mapping out a long-term program in preparation for the great day. In the *Pilot* for December 7, 1878, O'Reilly set forth the significance of the movement:

When the whole voting population of Ireland has felt the agitation and has answered at the polls by filling all offices with trusty men, we shall get a national expression from Ireland that will at last be formidable to England.

Before the New Departure was so precipitously launched, Devoy, Davitt, and Carroll appeared to have only general plans. They were anxious to found a newspaper and to bring over from Ireland speakers who would expound the new strategy. To tap new sources of revenue for propaganda and arms, they changed the name "Skirmishing Fund" to "National Fund," hoping thereby to convince rich Irish-Americans of the fund's respectability.

Much of Davitt's time during the lecture tour, which took him westward across the Mississippi, was taken up with Clan organizational problems. His letters written at this time—querulous and full of the complaints of a lecturer making one-night stands— bear out Devoy's later statements that Davitt was then keenly interested in preparing the ground for the anticipated political revolution. Had he at this time attempted to transform the New Departure into a movement passionately dedicated to land reform as its major objective, he would have been ostracized by the Clan. But so successful was he in revitalizing Clan camps that Carroll hoped he might continue the work rather than return to Ireland, where he was liable to arrest for conspiring with revolutionaries in violation of his ticket-of-leave.

Nevertheless, it is difficult to believe that Davitt could have long been absorbed exclusively in the stale intrigues and petty politics of the Clan na Gael. He was an intellectually alert man who soaked up ideas like a sponge. He must have been affected by the currents of radical social thought that swirled about every dusty American town he visited.

With the issuance of Devoy's telegram, the cat was out of the bag, and more positive planning was demanded of Devoy and company. Davitt upon returning to the East met with the Clan leaders and pledged himself to the program outlined in the New Departure telegram, while Devoy on his part agreed to join Davitt abroad in an effort to win over Parnell and the I.R.B.

leaders. In keeping with the broad purposes of the undertaking, they were careful to get the approval of O'Reilly and others in order that they might claim in conversations abroad that they represented Irish-American opinion.

Their mission was not an easy one. Rigorously doctrinaire nationalists on both sides of the Atlantic were scandalized by the New Departure. Their reading of Irish history assured them that any faith placed in parliamentarians resulted in disaster. The doctrinaires had shaped their lives in the image of Mitchel. Now they were being asked to forsake intransigence for involvement, and they were shaken.

Moreover, they had little faith in the tenant farmers. They considered them bereft of idealism and believed that any substantial improvement in their situation would make them forever indifferent to the high cause of national freedom. In the final speech of his American tour, given in Boston, December 8, 1878, Davitt addressed himself to this concern. In a moving passage he suggested the reasoning of the peasant when confronted with nationalist demands for help.

> The nationalist party tells me that when independence is won, I will no longer be at the mercy of an English landlord. . . . Yellow meal porridge [however] is a more substantial meal than visionary plenty. . . . [If the nationalists want my support] they must first show themselves . . . strong enough to stand between me and the power which a single Englishman wields over me.[7]

Land and other reforms were therefore indispensable preliminaries to any peasant commitment to the nationalists.

To quiet the storms of criticism, which threatened the frail lines of transatlantic cooperation that Devoy and Carroll had so laboriously strung, Devoy sent off another gloss in the form of a letter to the Dublin *Freeman's Journal*. In the *Herald* report the terms "combination," "union," and "alliance" had been used to define the projected relationship with the Parnellites. But in the second gloss he assured the orthodox that no abandonment of nationalist principle was contemplated and no alliance intended. The letter was written on December 11, 1878, the day Devoy sailed for France, where he was to join Davitt in an effort to persuade Parnell and the I.R.B. supreme council to form such an alliance.

Devoy and Davitt met with the I.R.B. supreme council in Paris on or about January 20, 1879. The four-day conference—dominated by the aging novelist, Charles Kickham—was disappointing to the advocates of change. Formal participation in parliamentary politics or land reform agitation was condemned as deviationism. Only nationalist activity to win control over local offices received the council's imprimatur.

But however much dogma lay with Kickham, power lay with Parnell; and the New Departure authors sought him out. They met with him in Boulogne on the French coast on March 7, 1879. This meeting was inconclusive, but Devoy's impression was that the Irish leader had no scruples against the use of force and no fixed opinions as to the measure of self-government that should be pursued. Devoy thought him an opportunist who would do what he had to do.

Meanwhile, trouble in County Mayo in the West of Ireland was reaching a crisis. During the two years previous there had been periodic demonstrations, led by friends of the *Irish World,* against rack rents and capricious evictions. Now, after a series of poor potato harvests, the people were hungry and desperate. Davitt became aware of this when he journeyed into Mayo, his native county, after the disappointing Paris meeting. Subsequently, he aided James Daly of the Connaught *Telegraph,* which had been following the *Irish World* line, and others in organizing the famous demonstration at Irishtown, County Mayo, on April 20, 1879. Some 15,000 people and 500 green-bannered horsemen were said to have been present there to demand fair play for the tenant farmer.

The Irishtown meeting marked a turning point. Not for some time would Davitt and Devoy openly quarrel but thereafter they would begin pulling in different directions. The Irishtown demonstration led in August of 1879 to the formation of the Land League of Mayo and in October to the Land League of Ireland. Into this work Davitt threw himself wholeheartedly; he became Ireland's foremost champion of land reform. In so doing he gradually moved away from the narrow nationalism of the New Departure into the broad stream of land and social reform then animating thoughtful humanitarians on both sides of the Atlantic. Of the two forces which we have said were thrown forward by the hard times of the 1870's—nationalism and the search for social justice—he became spokesman chiefly for the latter.

After the Irishtown demonstration, Davitt tried to get Parnell to accept leadership of the land movement. But the Squire of Avondale hung back until the spread of the agitation throughout Connaught forced his hand. Finally, at a meeting held on June 1, 1879, at Morison's Hotel, Dublin, he agreed to Davitt's entreaties. A week later he went down to a great gathering of tenant farmers held at Westport, County Mayo, where he advised them in memorable words to show the landlords that "you intend to hold a firm grip on your homesteads and lands."

According to Devoy, however, the Morison Hotel meeting did more than bring the great talents of Parnell into the land war. It also effected the grand alliance of Davitt, Devoy, and Parnell on the basis of the New Departure. Among other things, the three allegedly agreed that the Home Rule and land movements should not be detrimental to Fenianism and furthermore, that preparation for an armed uprising should go forward. In later years both Davitt and Parnell denied ever entering into such a binding agreement. The Morison Hotel conference, according to Davitt, simply provided for "an open participation in public movements by extreme men . . . in friendly rivalry with moderate nationalists."

That a conference conducted without written records in a hotel room would be subject to misunderstanding was perhaps inevitable. What is interesting is that each participant offered an interpretation that fitted the needs of his career as it unfolded. Parnell became, in 1880, the head of the Home Rule party, which was dedicated to winning lawful social and constitutional changes within the United Kingdom. His leadership would have been seriously impaired by an admission that he was intimately tied to American revolutionaries.

Devoy's reputation, on the other hand, was dependent upon his claim that he had a gentleman's agreement with Parnell that looked forward to revolution. Only an understanding of this kind would have justified Devoy's devotion to Parnell in the face of Fenian critics.

It is the informed judgment of most Irish historians that Parnell would never have entangled himself in arrangements so imprudent as those described by Devoy. Very likely they are right. There are, however, bits and pieces of evidence to be found in Devoy's collected letters that suggest some sort of an understanding.[8] But the most that we may conclude from this evidence is that Devoy and his associates in the United States *thought* Parnell had committed himself to their revolutionary schemes. Their hopes in this matter probably outran the facts. Parnell was a gifted diplomat, capable of winning support while retaining his own freedom of action. At any rate, the essential fact to bear in mind is that the Americans did bind themselves to Parnell. They would remain more or less loyal allies throughout the remainder of his career.

For Davitt, the denial of an alliance was of the greatest importance. His vast personal influence throughout the British Isles was dependent upon the public's image of him as a compassionate Christian reformer: the one-armed, self-made man who suffered the indignities of prison, yet emerged free of bitterness to take up the cause of the Irish poor and the poor everywhere by methods unstained by violence. It was perhaps concern for this image that explains Davitt's eagerness to defend himself before the Special Commission established by Parliament in 1888 to look into charges that Parnell was linked to the American revolutionaries, a defense many comrades thought unwise and in which Davitt was often less than frank. The Land League, he testified,

> was largely, not entirely, the offspring of thoughts and resolutions which whiled away many a dreary and tedious hour in political captivity. . . . It represented the triumph of what was forgiving over what was vengeful in my Celtic temperament.[9]

Whatever was or was not agreed upon at the Morison meeting, it is clear enough that Davitt was bound by the New Departure to a program aimed at political revolution and that the land reforms contemplated therein were definitely of secondary importance. Even during the first hectic days of organizing the Land League, Davitt devoted time to the work of running guns into Ireland and England in preparation for the goal he and Devoy had agreed upon. But it was not long before the Land League elevated Davitt to a position of greater influence than he had ever had before or would ever have again. Land reform then became his obsession, as it had long been Patrick Ford's; and the New Departure's political program became of secondary interest at best. If at the Morison Hotel conference Devoy had insisted upon subordinating the land movement to the New Departure, as he claimed, he was at least justified by subsequent events.

Davitt was an extraordinarily sensitive man, possessing, along with the finest qualities of heart and mind, perhaps too much of that Irish desire to please. And he was jealous of the epic that had sprung up about his name. His recollections, such as that quoted at the head of this chapter, contributed to the epic but did not do justice to the facts. He seemed almost unaware of how much the events of the early 1880's reshaped his life and thoughts. Perhaps this was inevitable. They were shattering events. They destroyed the old order and prepared the way for modern Ireland.

The attitudes of the Irish people on the American continent in the struggle between the tenant farmers of Ireland and their cruel and unrelentless oppressors has touched the hearts of the Irish exiles of Southwark, London.

Letter of THOMAS WALSH, Southwark, London, April 27, 1881, to Patrick Collins of Boston

CHAPTER SIX

The War for the Land of Ireland

I N 1880 Ireland hovered on the very edge of catastrophe. Six hundred thousand people in the seventeen counties of the West were estimated to be in the need of food to avoid starvation. Once again the authorities had been slow to respond to warnings that arose as agricultural prices plunged in the late 1870's and that became urgent after two years of bad potato harvests. It was chiefly the work of private charity agencies that kept Ireland going through the summer until the improved harvest of 1880 eased the situation. Ireland came very close to repeating the nightmare of the Great Famine.

But the reaction of the Irish people was very different from what it had been in Young Ireland's time. A new generation of Irishmen had come of age in England, Ireland, Scotland, and the United States. They had been raised on memories of the Great Hunger and were determined that its pattern of death and disintegration would not be repeated. The nationalism that had been so excitingly fresh to Young Ireland was bred in the bones of this new generation. Some were, like Davitt, of peasant origins, and all were closer in spirit to the people they would lead than Young Ireland had been. They were also tougher minded, free of the scruples (and many of the graces) of Young Ireland. Many had

learned the arts of debate and demagoguery in the Fenian movement. Journalism was a common profession among them. They
knew the techniques of propaganda and the sensibilities of
the reading public on both sides of the Atlantic.

The Land League was their instrument. They used it to maintain the peasant on the land in the face of ruinous rents and
evictions and, in conjunction with the Home Rule party, as a
battering-ram to break down the centuries-old commitment of the
British government to the Anglo-Irish landlords. The League's
history reveals how closely the nationalist adapted himself to the
peasant world, for the Land League's essential power lay in its
legitimatization of old Whiteboy techniques. The chief weapon
was the boycotting of rack-renters and land-grabbers—a formali-
zation of the ostracism customarily visited upon one who broke
the peasant code. The name derives from Captain Boycott, a
much-disliked County Mayo land agent who, in 1880, was effec-
tively isolated by the local people until his nerve broke, and he
fled to England. Boycotting simply channeled traditional village
hostilities into nonviolent forms. It existed side by side with older
kinds of terrorism: cattle maimings, night burnings and shootings,
and assassination. Though the League tried to discourage these
acts of violence, they nevertheless contributed to the pressures
that League leaders brought to bear upon the government.

There was also a new generation of Englishmen for whom the
old doctrines of *laissez faire* were no longer so sacrosanct. It was
adherence to these economic dogmas—not maliciousness, as the
Irish thought—which had inhibited the British government's
efforts to deal with the Great Famine. Hard times and unrest
among workers who now had the vote encouraged a new willingness to reappraise the possibilities of government intervention in
the social and economic order. The Conservative party under
Disraeli's leadership from 1874 to 1880 had sought distractions
from these problems in imperialist adventures abroad. But the
Liberals who held power after 1880, with Gladstone as Prime
Minister, had no choice but to face the issues raised by the hard

times. By the Land Act of 1870, which reversed the policy begun with the Encumbered Estates Act (1849) of establishing a free market in Irish land, Gladstone had already shown a willingness to move away from *laissez faire*. The Land League would force him further down this road.

The food crisis in Ireland, widely publicized by American journalists, quickly won for the Irish people American sympathy and financial aid. Mass meetings to raise funds were held in most major American cities in the fall of 1879, and at that time the American Catholic hierarchy began a series of appeals to Catholics for help.

Thus Parnell had a ready-made audience when he traveled to the United States late in 1879 to raise funds and win friends for the Land League. Between his arrival in January, 1880, and his departure in March of that year he covered over 16,000 miles, spoke in sixty-two cities, and had the rare privilege of addressing a joint session of Congress. His tour was instrumental in raising over $300,000 for famine relief and Land League agitation in the first six months of 1880.

Parnell's insistence upon collecting money for the League as well as for relief offended many Americans. James Gordon Bennett, proprietor of the New York *Herald*, declared in a quarrel with Parnell that the Irish land question was not an American concern, and he set up his own rival fund. But Parnell insisted that the famine was an outgrowth of the iniquitous Irish land system, and he took every opportunity to drive the point home. In his speech before Congress he laid out the arguments in favor of compulsory sale of the great Irish landed estates to the farmers who worked them, and was careful to cite John Bright, the greatly admired English Liberal, as favoring this system of ownership.

The calling of a British general election forced Parnell to cut short his tour. Escorted by the Irish-American 69th Regiment and looking, as some said, like a king, he embarked for home on

March 10, 1880. Just before sailing he hastily called a group together at the New York Hotel to lay plans for an American Land League. Thenceforth, the Irish land question was an American as well as an Irish issue.

The American Land League fulfilled its function of providing the home organization with money and moral support, but its history was never a happy one. From the outset its members were divided by the hopes and tensions that had arisen in the 1870's.

For Patrick Ford and his followers the land agitation offered them a unique opportunity to carry out their principles governing land use. They believed that only nationalization of the land of Ireland would regenerate that nation and make of it the model community which Thomas Davis had wanted to build. Ireland then would be an example for the United States to follow. For John Devoy and the Clan na Gael the League was at best an instrument with which to arouse Irish national feeling in preparation for carrying out the New Departure program; at worst, a diversion of energies which would subvert the New Departure.

There was a third group, much more difficult to define, whom we shall call conservatives. They had no particular ax to grind; they were held together by their fear of the other factions. The Land League was simply an expression of their nationalism, of the ties that bound them to Ireland and to America. They wanted to aid the Irish farmer but not at the expense of doing an injury to their standing in America. Parnell had been feted by the governors of Indiana and Illinois; he had spoken before Congress. Noted Americans like Wendell Phillips and Henry Ward Beecher had endorsed his cause. The conservatives were anxious not to lose this approval, and they feared that the plans of Ford and Devoy would have that result. Their spokesmen were often Catholic clergymen who condemned the conspiracies of Devoy and the social radicalism of the *Irish World*.

Conflict among these factions was apparent from the beginning. In the New York Hotel meeting to establish the American League, Parnell had proposed that each American branch forward money directly to Dublin, thus ensuring that the balance of power would lie across the Atlantic. To this the Clan na Gael objected. They were not prepared to permit the American movement to become the tail of a kite. They wanted a centralized American organization in control of its own finances. The conservatives, however, feared the consequences of such control. Their concern may be traced back to the previous October, when a Devoy-inspired manifesto (the National Fund Manifesto) called upon Irish-Americans to ready themselves for the revolution that would inevitably arise out of the land agitation. The Manifesto made a powerful appeal:

> Surviors of '47' . . . does the memory of the hunger pang, the pestilence, the reeking emigrant ship and the ghastly fever shed arouse no righteous indignation in your souls . . . can you contemplate a repetition of these scenes . . . ?

Bishop Hendricken of Providence, Rhode Island, promptly denounced the Manifesto and warned Catholics against turning money over to the National Fund.

The issue was joined at the Land League's inaugural convention held at Treanor Hall, New York City, on May 18 and 19, 1880. The delegates divided on the question of centralization versus branch autonomy. Devoy and O'Reilly argued for centralization and American control over the funds, pointing out that only in this way could there be unified American action and strength sufficient to keep the movement together, should it be splintered in Ireland. The priests present and a number of veterans of earlier nationalist movements, perhaps recalling how money had been misappropriated in the past, wanted each branch to act independently in collecting and forwarding funds. Eventually a compromise was reached. The constitution agreed upon provided that all money forwarded to Ireland go through the office of the central treasurer; then that office was entrusted to the Reverend Lawrence Walsh, a priest from Waterbury, Connecticut. At the second convention, held in Buffalo, in January, 1881, the conservatives had their way and revised the constitution so as to permit branches to forward money directly to Dublin if their members chose to do so.

Meanwhile, Patrick Ford had entered the field on his own. He had reserved judgment about the Irish agitation until Parnell went down to Westport, County Mayo, in June, 1879, and committed himself to the movement. As the crisis developed in the fall of 1879 and winter of 1880, Ford's enthusiasm mounted. Davitt was commissioned to send a weekly cable to the *Irish World*, and the paper gave up much of its American news in the interest of making the Land League an instrument of abolishing private property in land. The League leaders in Ireland were counseling the peasantry to refuse payment of rents considered unjust, but the *Irish World* went beyond this by demanding that the tenant farmers refuse payment of any rent whatsoever.

Ford played no part in the Treanor Hall proceedings that established the American Land League. Instead, he organized his own League, drawing up a constitution that called for the transmission of funds to Dublin by way of the *Irish World* office. Each week he published an account of the sums sent in and listed the names of the donors. In this way the *Irish World* became the greatest single channel of Land League funds. By the fall of 1882 more than $343,000 had been dispatched to the home organization.[1]

The British government made an effort to ban the *Irish World* from Ireland but without much success. In addition to a paid Irish circulation of 20,000, additional copies were circulated abroad under subsidy from the special "Spread the Light" fund Ford had set up. More than $7,600 was raised for this purpose and over 450,000 copies of the paper were said to have been distributed throughout the course of the agitation. James Redpath, the old abolitionist who had taken up the Land League cause, found the *Irish World* widely influential during his first Irish tour in 1880.

The nature of the paper's influence, however, is difficult to determine. Its central teaching—that the land belonged to the people and they were under no obligation to pay rent for its use—was a highly abstract proposition. It derived from eighteenth-century thought and drew strength from the findings of Victorian scholarship, which asserted that in all early societies land was held in common and private property was unknown. History as well as philosophy seemed to be on the side of the *Irish World*. By encouraging the peasant to withhold rents the paper was fostering restoration of the ancient communal practices of the Gael. Many historians of the Land League have believed that memory of the communal past survived among the peasantry, sustaining them in their fight against landlordism.

The Irish tenant farmer, of course, was not confronting a theory but a terrible reality; eviction followed upon failure to pay the rent. Moreover, it was a reality that had bred fear into the bone of many generations. A. M. Sullivan perhaps exaggerated when he declared that nowhere in Ireland "will you find any trace of the idea that the landlord is not entitled to his rent. That right is universally, cheerfully given";[2] but the Land League organizers appear to have found it difficult to persuade the people to tamper with the rents. As a John Hurley reported from Kilnarovanagh, County Cork:

> The thought never possessed them [the tenant farmers] that they had the greatest and only just claims to the land . . . or that they would be justified in demanding from the land robber any part of the hereditary privileges he had so long mercilessly held.[3]

Not the folk memory of a collectivist golden age, but fears inherited from the past mixed with hopes for better days seem to have motivated the tenant farmers of Ireland.

It seems likely that the democratic indignation of the *Irish World* rather than its theories commended it to the agitator and tenant farmer. Like James Redpath, who, during his Irish tour, habitually lectured the peasantry on the undemocratic behavior of tipping their hats to landlords, the *Irish World* was probably most effective in encouraging the people to defy their masters. Letters from obscure Irish agitators to the *Irish World* in the fall of 1880 bear witness to peasant habits and the paper's influence.

> The people are beginning to recognize that they are not an inferior race. . . . The mean cringing gnome . . . is just becoming upright and manly. . . . I have got a rule passed in one branch that in the future anyone taking off his hat for any man save a clergyman be at once expelled.

The slogan "the land for the people" had unhappy implications both for the Irish tenant farmer and for conservatives among the American Irish. It meant that the Irish farm laborer, who was badly exploited by the tenant farmer, had as much right to the land as his exploiter. It also meant that the landless poor of America, the restless wage earners of the cities, were being denied their natural rights by the prevailing economic system. "The cause of the poor in Donegal," said the *Irish World*, "is the cause of the factory slave in Fall River."

Throughout the fall and winter of 1880, when famine still threatened Ireland, there was widespread approval in the United States for the counsel given the peasantry to withhold the rents in order to provide themselves with food and clothing. General Rosecrans of Civil War fame was among those who endorsed this advice. Fanny Parnell, the beautiful sister of the Irish leader, wrote an enormously popular poem at her home in Bordentown, New Jersey, that became the "Marseillaise" of the movement:

Oh, by the God who made us all—
The Seigneur and the serf—
Rise up! and swear this day to hold
Your own green Irish turf;
Rise up! and plant your feet as men
Where now you crawl as slaves,
And make the harvest fields your camps,
Or make of them your graves.

By the spring of 1881, however, conservatives in America had begun to suffer doubts about the wisdom of this counsel. The *Irish World* by then had made it obvious that it was not going to compromise with what it called the "great blasphemy"; that it was determined to employ the League against the "railroad thief" (Rosecrans was one, according to Stephen Dillaye, greenbacker and *Irish World* staff member) and American land speculators of every description.

Charges that the *Irish World* was communistic came from many quarters, especially from the Catholic clergy. Patrick Collins of Boston, who was elected president of the American Land League at Buffalo, joined with his friend John Boyle O'Reilly in a long and ultimately successful effort to break Patrick Ford's influence.

But for some time Ford profited from the divisions among his opponents. Antagonism between the conservatives and the extreme nationalists was open and bitter at the Buffalo gathering. Devoy was angered by the constitutional change that authorized local League branches to communicate directly with Dublin. Shortly afterward he advised the branches under his influence to freeze their funds. Other extremists wanted to smash the League.

Devoy broke with Ford in April, 1881, after the *Irish World* revealed the history of the Skirmishing Fund in a way embarrassing to the Clan. But a mutual distaste for Ford felt by conservatives and extreme nationalists was not yet great enough to bring them together. As a consequence the leaders in Ireland were forced, despite Collins' repeated complaints, to defer to the *Irish World* editor as to a rich patron.

In the first year and a half Michael Davitt was the great personality of the land war—the William Lloyd Garrison, as James Redpath called him, of the Irish people. All factions of the American Irish looked to him for leadership. In May, 1880, he had come over to the United States to participate in the Treanor Hall work of laying the American League foundations and had then been elected secretary of the organization. Shortly afterward he embarked upon a speaking tour that took him to the West Coast and back. During this tour he irritated Devoy by advising Land League branches to forward their funds directly to Dublin or by any major channel that appealed to them: the national treasurer, the Boston *Pilot,* or the *Irish World.* The weakness of the American League's central organization undoubtedly influenced Davitt to give this advice, but he may also have been wary of giving the Clan na Gael an opportunity to control the flow of money.

Davitt's intentions at this time remain obscure. Shortly before leaving for the United States he had been removed from the I.R.B. supreme council, and no doubt he was already beginning to move away from conventional Fenianism toward the path of social reform. In the period before coming to the United States for his second visit, he had been serving as a weekly correspondent for the *Irish World;* and as he later stated, he may already have been persuaded that land nationalization was the only proper solution for the Irish land question. There is little evidence for this, however, in the speeches given during this tour.

The chief difference between Devoy and Davitt at this time appears to have been in the value each placed upon the Land League. As for Devoy there was a strong note of regret that the preliminary build-up to the New Departure program had taken the form of the Land League. He still insisted, as he had in Brooklyn's New Park Theater in October, 1878, that nothing much in the way of land reform could be expected until Ireland had its own parliament. Davitt, on the other hand, believed that the Land League's enormous strength would force from England a radical alteration of the land system. Once that was accomplished, the Irish could then move toward the political revolution outlined in the New Departure. In September, 1880, at Virginia City, Nevada, he told an audience of miners, "We can afford to put away the harp until we have abolished poverty, mud cabins, and social degradation from Ireland. Then it will be time enough to think of the best means of achieving independence for Ireland."[4]

Davitt returned to Ireland in December 1880 as the land war

was approaching a crisis. By then the Land League had firmly established itself as the effective ruling force throughout most of the country. To deal with it the alarmed Liberal government was preparing to introduce in the forthcoming parliamentary session a coercion bill that would empower authorities to arrest on sight any "reasonably suspected person" and, as a balancing measure, a land reform bill that would pacify the peasantry.

As Davitt realized, two dangers faced the League in this circumstance. Coercion might arouse the extremists to premature revolution, or the land reform bill might win over the moderates within the League and so split the movement. To avert the latter, he wanted to call a national convention that would, he assumed, reject any compromise on the land question. To avert the former, he called upon the extremists to act with caution.

> In case the Government resorts to dragooning the people . . . something should be done by way of retaliation *in England*— but nothing should be done until the Government takes the initiative [he wrote to Devoy]. All we want is to be let alone for a few months longer by the Government *and the Nationalists,* and we will have Ireland in such a state of organization as she never was in before.[5]

Gladstone, however, did not give the Irish agitators this period of grace. On February 3, 1881, Davitt was arrested and imprisoned on the charge of violating his ticket-of-leave. When news of this reached Parnell and his followers, who had been conducting a month-long filibuster in the House of Commons to block the Coercion bill, they created such turmoil in the House that they were ejected. The crisis that the New Departure authors had anticipated was now at hand. Parnell was urged by the Davitt faction within the League to withdraw permanently from Parliament and intensify the land war by adopting a general strike against rents. Parnell prudently avoided adopting this course and instead began a long and skillful withdrawal of his forces to a more conservative position.

Even had he been more radically inclined, the situation in Ireland in the late winter and spring of 1881 was by no means favorable. The American League was torn by bickering which restricted the flow of funds. Up to January, 1881, less than $5,000 had been transmitted from Father Walsh, the League's national treasurer, to Dublin. Greater sums had passed through other American channels, but even Patrick Ford, with his proven methods of raising money, had forwarded only $43,707 up to this point. The Liberal government's imprisonment of Davitt aroused greater American interest in the movement than his lecture tour had. Resolutions of sympathy for him were adopted by the state legislatures of Iowa, Maine, New Jersey, and Texas. Thereafter, membership in the American League increased rapidly. But it would be a long time before the wounds opened at the Buffalo convention (held a month before Davitt's arrest) were healed.

Moreover, with the Coercion Act's passage in late February, the League in Ireland began to lose control over the peasantry. William Mackey Lomasney, after exploring the situation in Ireland, assured Devoy in a letter dated March 31 that the time was not ripe for revolution. Lomasney was a fearless man, and, certainly, he was not disposed to take a more conservative view of things than Parnell.

The American extremists, nevertheless, still retained hopes of carrying out the New Departure program in 1882. In two letters written to Devoy in the spring of 1881, John O'Leary refers in veiled language to a plan the two had discussed in Philadelphia in 1880. In the first there are several references to a plan for "'82." Later in a letter dated April 22, 1881, the plan is designated as "next year's work." O'Leary, spiritually a Young Irelander, critical of the land movement and terrorism, said of the plan for 1882: "I then and now believed [sic] that it was the most important work we could do and hence, I'd do more to carry it out than almost anything else."

In that spring of 1881 emissaries from the Clan na Gael met with Parnell apparently to discuss, among other things, preparations for the following year. In a letter of February 18, Lomasney told of his conversations with Parnell:

> I feel that he is eminently deserving of our support and that he means to go as far as we do in pushing this business. I had Knox [John O'Leary] also go and see him. He told him the same as myself, that as soon as he secured the means he would start in business with us and smash up the opposition firm.

The other contact was made by Henri Le Caron, the British secret agent, then in the Clan's confidence. He, too, assured Devoy of Parnell's willingness to cooperate. Especially interesting was the reaction of the Chicago trial lawyer and Clansman, W. J. Hynes, when he was informed of Le Caron's interview. What is pertinent here is not Le Caron's statement, whose accuracy we may doubt, but Hynes' response: "I have no doubt but the cooperation of Osborne [John O'Connor, the secretary of the I.R.B. supreme council] and his friends can be secured, particularly in view of the possibilities which the programme for '82 will offer."[6]

These negotiations never bore the fruit intended, but they did renew the basis for cooperation with Parnell—cooperation of the greatest importance when conflict with the radical social reformers erupted in the spring of 1882.

Gladstone's sweeping land reforms, which he first introduced to the House in April, 1881, provided the issue that progressively arrayed the extreme nationalists and the moderates against the social radicals. Departing from cherished Liberal principles, the Land Act of 1881 was based on the "Three F's," which Isaac Butt, and earlier the Tenant Right leagues, had championed: fixity of tenure, fair rents established by land courts, and free sale of improvements made to holdings. As the extraordinarily complex bill was undergoing debate in the House, the *Irish World* in the United States and Davitt's followers in Ireland made savage attacks upon it. They saw nothing in it of advantage to the farm laborers, and were determined to go ahead with their plans to wipe out landlordism. They wanted a general strike against rents. They received an unexpected windfall in April, when the Bishop of Meath, Dr. Thomas Nulty, issued a pastoral letter assuring his flock that the land of every country was the common property of the people because the "Creator who made it transferred it as voluntary gift to them."

Parnell was in a difficult position. Evictions were increasing rapidly, jumping to 5,262 for the second quarter of 1881, and Whiteboy terrorism was keeping pace with them. Farm laborers in the South of Ireland, especially in County Cork, were becoming more insistent upon fairer treatment from the tenant farmers. The social radicals wanted the bill rejected; the moderates were all for it. Parnell decided to stall for time.

When the Irish Land League convened in Dublin on April 22, the Home Rule leader sought to placate the radicals by calling for additions to the bill that would, among other things, provide subsidies for the building of dwellings for farm laborers. But Thomas Brennan, who then served the *Irish World* as correspondent, warned that acceptance of the bill in any form would mean loss of American aid. After assuring the delegates that they were working for humanity and were "watched by toilers of every land," Brennan said significantly that soon they would have to take up the political question. "The centenary time of memorable history is here. If our friends in Ulster will only remember Dungannon with the demand for free land we can associate with them in the demand for liberty."[7] By unanimous vote the convention adopted a resolution to the effect that the peasantry would be satisfied with nothing less than the abolition of landlordism. Nevertheless, this generality left the Home Rule party free to support the government bill or not as they pleased.

Thereafter, Parnell tacked according to the wind, trying to maintain control of the various factions of Parnellites, while the bill itself proceeded through Parliament to become law on August 22. When the Irish League convened again in Dublin in September, Parnell's problems were somewhat less acute because most of the major radicals had been arrested under the Coercion Act and lodged in Dublin's Kilmainham prison. But Ford still maintained his influence over the American movement, and he gathered his strength to force the Irish leaders into resisting the Land Act. Messages from the United States urging them to take up a general strike against rents deluged the delegates. Parnell, however, was able to get a wise compromise adopted. The Land Act was to be neither accepted nor rejected. Instead the League would test it by bringing certain selected cases before the Land Courts established under the act to determine whether or not they would fix truly equitable rents.

After winning this fight for moderation, Parnell apparently felt it necessary to mask his move with a series of incendiary speeches in Ireland calculated to appeal to the radicals and hold them in line. Gladstone was thoroughly exasperated and, in a thunderous speech at Leeds in Yorkshire on October 7, 1881, warned Parnell that the government's patience was all but exhausted. Parnell replied at Wexford with a deliberately defiant and insulting speech that he must have known would cause his arrest under the Coercion Act. On October 13 he was taken into custody and sent to join his lieutenants in Kilmainham prison. Four days later the imprisoned Irish leaders instructed the tenant farmers in the famous No Rent Manifesto to withhold the rents from the landlords. The *Irish World* was exultant. "You have landlordism by the throat," it assured the imprisoned leaders. "Do not let go of your grip until you have strangled it."

Issuing the No Rent Manifesto was the last official act of the Land League of Ireland. Shortly afterward it was suppressed by the government. But the movement itself was far from dead. The Ladies Land League, which Davitt had organized for just such an emergency, took command under the leadership of Parnell's fanatical sister, Anna. The movement lived on, too, in the United States, where the conflict between nationalists and social reformers that had been simmering since the 1870's reached a crisis in the winter and spring of 1882.

Mr. Davitt is the dupe of his American friends, and his scheme is a scheme, not so much for the regeneration of Ireland as for making that unhappy country a corpus vile *on which to try the experiment of American communism.*

Dublin *Review*, July, 1882

Henry George and his school care nothing about Irish nationality . . . but the Irish people want Irish nationality.

Boston *Pilot*, July 1, 1882

CHAPTER SEVEN

The Triumph of Nationalism

THE English government could suppress the Land League, but it could not check the rich flow of American dollars into the Land League treasury in Paris, where it had been established in the winter of 1881. Patrick Egan, a Dublin flour merchant and former member of the I.R.B. supreme council, was a remarkably efficient treasurer. From his headquarters at the Brighton Hotel, he dispatched money to Ireland to keep the agitation going and propaganda to the United States to keep the money coming. He prudently avoided the numerous opportunities afforded him to enter into quarrels with the clamoring American factions.

Meanwhile, Ireland's two great leaders, Parnell and Davitt, were spending their prison hours—Parnell in Kilmainham and Davitt in Portland prison, Dorsetshire—meditating on what to do next. Parnell decided to move to the right and seek concessions from the English Liberals in return for calling off the land war. Davitt decided to strike leftward and go on with the land war in the anticipation that it would result in adoption of land nationalization as the solution to Ireland's problems. In reaching his decision the former Fenian was strongly influenced by Henry George's *Progress and Poverty*, the book which better than any other expressed the era's yearning for a more just social order. The crisis in the spring of 1882 was dominated by these three personalities: Parnell, who stood for nationalism; George, who spoke for humanitarian social reform; and Davitt, who tried to stand for both.

The crisis forced Irish-Americans to consider their situation. Did they want to follow Davitt and George in pursuit of the perfect social order? Or did they want Irish solidarity, that source of strength in American life and force with which to win America's respect?

The depression of the 1870's and the famine in Ireland had prepared the popular mind for Henry George's great social analysis, whose publication coincided with Parnell's visit in January, 1880. Among reformers, that proud and jealous breed, *Progress and Poverty* made an immediate impression. Though neither the doctrinaire socialist nor the greenbacker could agree completely with George that land monopoly was the major source of social evil and land nationalization the cure, they were profoundly moved by his indictment of contemporary society. He stirred their minds and hopes as had the land agitation in Ireland.

George's association with the Irish was early and intimate. And it was not, as is often thought, the product of an Irish delusion that George was a nationalist. His appeal was to the radical wing of the Land League. The work of the Land Reform League of California, with which George was connected, along with Judge James Maguire and other Irish before coming to the East, had attracted favorable comment from the *Irish World*. And this journal was one of the first to take him up after publication of *Progress and Poverty*. In August of 1880, George was invited to Ford's home on Staten Island and that November, Ford introduced him to Davitt. According to the *Irish World* editor, Davitt endorsed everything George had to say about land nationalization, but wondered "how is that to be effected in Ireland under British domination."[1] Davitt promised to push George's book in Great Britain, and when he retired to the solitude of Portland, he took a copy of the book with him to puzzle over its significance for Ireland.

As for George, he left little doubt about the significance of Ireland for him. In the *Irish Land Question,* brought out in the spring of 1881, he emphasized that the Irish movement for political independence was irrelevant to Ireland's problems. Private property in land, not English iniquity, was at the root of Ireland's misery. Since the land belonged solely to the people, the "Three F's" were "three frauds," and so also was the solution of peasant proprietorship, which would transfer land monopoly from the English to the Irish, without benefit to the landless classes. The solution was to nationalize the land by means of a tax that would restore to society the rental value of the land, a value created by society but now appropriated by landlords.

Somewhat discomfited by George's too easy dismissal of Ireland's political ambitions, Ford nevertheless found the land tax proposal attractive. It would achieve the benefits of land collectivization while at the same time keeping to a minimum government intervention in the social and economic order. The *Irish World* editor did not share George's faith in free trade, nor did he abandon his own belief that interest as well as rent was robbery. It was sufficient for him that "between the covers of *Progress and Poverty* there is enough seed thought to revolutionize the world."[2]

George was a popular speaker before radical Land League groups, whose members agreed with him that the land fight should be lifted out of the narrowness of national recrimination onto the high ground of the land for all people everywhere. In the spring of 1881, he made a speaking tour through New England and Canada under the auspices of Ford's Land League branches, and then in October he sailed for Ireland to serve there as the *Irish World* correspondent.

Henry George's excursion to Ireland was the boldest effort yet made by Ford to dominate the land movement, but circumstances were by no means propitious. The No Rent Manifesto was issued while George was on the Atlantic, and upon his arrival at

Queenstown he learned that the Land League had been suppressed. The peasantry were flocking to the Land Courts in defiance of Anna Parnell's Ladies Land League, and opposition to Ford was building up in America.

The No Rent Manifesto was the divisive issue. According to the *Irish World,* the Manifesto fully endorsed Ford's radical theories. In the judgment of conservatives and the revolutionary nationalists, it was only a tactical weapon employed to win the release from prison of Parnell and his lieutenants. "The man or party or paper," said John Boyle O'Reilly, "that would advise Irish tenants to pay no rent under any circumstances is either a fool or a rogue." Caught between these struggling factions, whose disagreements they only party understood, were three representatives of the movement in Ireland: T. P. O'Connor, Tim Healy, and Father Eugene Sheehy, a fiery priest who had spent the summer in Kilmainham. The three had come to the United States after Parnell's imprisonment. O'Connor and Healy sympathized with the conservatives, but they realized Ford's power. Up to November, 1881, the *Irish World* had contributed over $166,000 to the League, as compared with $131,923 forwarded from the official League's headquarters. And Ford promised that future contributions would make those of the past appear "but a drop in the bucket" if Ireland kept faith with the No Rent Manifesto.

To achieve unity at this time of difficulty, Ford and Collins, after considerable jealous haggling, agreed to join with the three Irish representatives in calling for delegates from all Irish-American societies to convene in Chicago at the end of November. Ford was hopeful that the convention would endorse his principles. The Clan na Gael delegates were anxious that the convention approve its old proposal for a centralized Irish-American institution. "We need one governing body and one treasury," declared John Devoy's newly founded *Irish Nation.* "We want an Irish-American movement that can speak in the name of our whole race and its work must not be confined to the interests of any one class of our people at home."[3] In this way

Devoy hoped to wrest control of the movement from Ford and direct its destinies in the interests of the New Departure.

The convention met in McCormack's Hall, Chicago, on November 30. Eight hundred and forty-five delegates were present for the three-day meeting.

The balance of power in the convention lay with the conservatives. They joined forces with the Clan na Gael, which won control over most of the convention committees, to frustrate the ambitions of Ford. The No Rent Manifesto was endorsed as a political expedient, without reference to its social and philosophical implications. And together the conservatives and the *Irish World* followers forced the Clan to accept a compromise on its desire to create a centralized Irish-American body. Devoy had to be satisfied with a committee of seven, which would look into the possibilities of forming a union of all Irish-American societies. The *Irish Nation* professed to have high hopes for this arrangement: "The Irish nation in America is no longer a horde of clans and warring factions . . . It is now a nation in fact as well as in name. It has now a representative government to give effect to its will . . ."[4] But opposition from Collins and the Catholic clergy soon rendered the committee powerless.

From the standpoint of the Irish delegates, the convention's work was most satisfactory. Moderation had prevailed, and $250,000 had been pledged by St. Patrick's Day to carry on the movement in Ireland. (By the first week in March over $108,000 of the sum pledged had been received by Egan in Paris). Fear that by a row they would disgrace themselves in American eyes was the centripetal force that held the delegates together.

The convention had shown its conservative temper by refusing to seat delegates from a Chicago socialist club. But such were the implications of the No Rent Manifesto that it was not easy to disassociate the land movement from radicalism. On January 30, 1882, twelve thousand representatives of the trade and labor unions of New York City met at Cooper Union to endorse the Manifesto. The speech of the evening was made by Louis Post, editor of *Truth*, Henry George disciple, and future Assistant Secretary of Labor under President Wilson.

> I am told that the Irish cause is a menace to the rights of property. So it is, as the Revolutionary War was a menace to the rights of property. . . . As the anti-slavery agitation was a menace to the rights of property. [The Kilmainham prisoners are leaders in a] new revolution which cannot be confined between the coasts of Ireland . . . but which will grow . . . until it sweeps the civilized world, terminating in . . . the banishment of involuntary poverty from the face of the earth.[5]

Many conservative Americans were disturbed by the Chicago convention. The distinction made there between the No Rent Manifesto as a political expedient and as a declaration of radical principles escaped them. Like Bishop McQuaid of Rochester, who denounced both the Manifesto and the Clan na Gael, they saw little difference between the political radicalism of the Clan and the social radicalism of the *Irish World*. In Cleveland, where Bishop Gilmour had long been at odds with the extreme nationalists, the conflict became scandalous. The formation of a ladies branch of the Land League appalled him. He thought it destructive of female modesty, and in a Sunday sermon on May 21, 1882, he let his views be known. The lady president of the branch in turn said flatly that "we do not want Scotch dictation by Bishop Gilmour." Subsequently, the Bishop declared excommunicated any female patriots who participated in the condemned organization. The ladies, nevertheless, continued with their labors and some urged boycotting the Bishop.[6] Elsewhere, priests who denounced the convention and the Manifesto were boycotted by their parishioners.

As dissension and scandal increased, League membership dropped off. The number of active Land League branches decreased in the late winter and spring of 1882 from 900 to 500, representing a loss of membership from perhaps 45,000 to 25,000. Conservatives who remained in the movement explained that their approval of the No Rent Manifesto should not be construed as hostility to the rights of private property in the United States.

Throughout the course of this debate the original backers of the New Departure struggled to regain some measure of control over the movement. John Boyle O'Reilly favored dropping the land agitation in favor of a concerted effort to win Home Rule in 1882. No less than Ford he was an admirer of Henry George, but he was not prepared to support social reform at the expense of Irish-American solidarity. An article of his in the *American Catholic Quarterly Review* for December, 1881, outlining the case for focusing efforts upon the Home Rule fight, was widely criticized as an abandonment of the imprisoned Irish leaders. O'Reilly thereupon pointed out in the *Pilot* for December 17, 1881, that Davitt had never intended the League to do anything more than it had already accomplished—win over the tenant farmers to nationalism. It was now time, he said, in words quoted earlier in this work, to pursue the New Departure's original intention of celebrating "the centennial of 1782 by a unanimous demand for the government of Ireland by the Irish."

For John Devoy these were especially difficult days. He saw his plans menaced from all sides. And with a Lenin-like intensity he castigated all who deviated from the line laid down in 1878-79. In the late winter of 1882 the *Irish Nation* lashed out at O'Reilly, for the New Departure had declared Home Rule unworthy of nationalist support; at Patrick Egan in Paris, who was accused of favoring Ford over the Clan na Gael; at John Finerty in Chicago, whose recently founded *Citizen* argued that the American Irish were obligated to follow wherever the Dublin leaders led them. The paper's greatest fury was vented upon Patrick Ford, the apostle of humanitarianism. An *Irish Nation* editorial for March 4, 1882, revealed Devoy's anxieties and the line he would force all to follow:

> What is our goal, world revolution for all humanity? Then we are lunatics. . . . Humanity is busy elsewhere. . . . The

next step forward . . . must be in the direction of Irish
nationality, and that step can only be taken when the people
of Ireland decide that the time has come for taking it. . . .
The logical consequences of the No Rent policy as preached
by the *Irish World*, are an abandonment of Ireland's national
hopes, the violation of Michael Davitt's and Parnell's solemn
pledges and an incentive to premature conflicts.

With the advent of spring the situation was eased. At a Land
League convention held in Washington on April 12, 1882, the
Clan patched up its differences with the conservatives. Though
only 250 delegates representing 200 Land League branches were
present, they were in agreement upon the necessity of blocking
the *Irish World's* humanitarian program. James Mooney, an Irish-
born real estate broker from Buffalo and a Clansman, was elected
president. With his confidence in the future restored, Devoy
urged his followers to forward once again their funds to Father
Walsh, who still served as the American League treasurer.

Meanwhile, events were taking shape in Ireland that would
test the strength of the forces in the United States hostile to
Patrick Ford and Henry George. Two days before the Washington Convention met, Parnell, moving to the right, began the negotiations with Gladstone that would in May culminate in the
Kilmainham Pact. By this agreement the Irish leader committed
himself to bringing the near-revolutionary land agitation to an
end in return for additional parliamentary legislation helpful to
the tenant farmers and a termination of coercion. In accordance
with this agreement, Parnell and others were released from Kilmainham on May 2. Ignorant of the conditions upon which Parnell was released, the *Irish Nation* was jubilant. "A memorable
day . . . it will mark the turning point of the tide of adversity."

Unfortunately, the tide had not yet reached flood; troubles of
all kinds lay ahead. On May 6, while a gay Parnell was escorting
Davitt to London from Portland prison, a group of assassins—the
Invincibles, as it was later determined—stabbed to death Lord
Frederick Cavendish, Ireland's newly appointed Chief Secretary,
and Thomas Burke, the Undersecretary, as they were strolling in

Dublin's Phoenix Park. The news threw Davitt and the usually self-disciplined Parnell into a panic. The latter came close to resigning his leadership, but was dissuaded from doing so by Gladstone. Instead, the Irish leaders drew up a press release repudiating any responsibility for the crime and calling for punishment for the assassins. Collins, O'Reilly and others in the United States followed this line, but Devoy refused to endorse what he called the "gush of raising money for informers." Not long afterward Michael Davitt gave Irish-Americans an even more disturbing shock than the Phoenix Park murders.

During his imprisonment in Portland, Davitt had mulled over the question of land nationalization, reading and rereading *Progress and Poverty*, and studying in detail the agricultural and financial statistics of Ireland. One of the first requests he made of Parnell upon leaving prison was permission to use Land League funds to publish a cheap edition of George's book for distribution throughout Great Britain. Then on May 21, against Parnell's wishes, Davitt presided over a Henry George meeting held in Manchester in the North of England.

There in the capital city of English liberalism, the Irish reformer gave assurances that he would go on with the land agitation in order to achieve a more fundamental solution of the Irish land question than was offered by peasant proprietorship. He was aware that he was challenging the aristocratic Parnell, and his justification for doing so was extraordinary for its pathos:

But humble and obscure though my origins may be—the son of an Irish peasant who was refused shelter in an Irish workhouse by an Irish landlord, the son of an Irish mother, who had to beg through English streets for me—humble as that origin may be, the memory of my mother made me swear [that] Irish landlords and English misgovernment in Ireland shall find in me a sleepless and incessant opponent.[7]

After the Manchester speech the cry went up from both sides of the Atlantic that Davitt had sold out Parnell for Henry George. In the United States both conservatives and extreme nationalists on the committee of seven, which the Chicago convention had established, got off a cable to Parnell assuring him of Irish-America's support. As for George—still serving as the *Irish World*'s Dublin correspondent—he was irritated but confident. "I know what they din into his [Davitt's] ears," the reformer wrote to Patrick Ford. " 'George has captured you for the *Irish World.*' But whatever happens now, Davitt will be to those moderates . . . a bull in a china shop."

George's judgment was confirmed when on June 6, before embarking for the United States on the steamer *Germania,* Davitt made a sensational speech in Liverpool. There he at last defined what he meant by the slogan "the land for the people" and came out flatly for land nationalization. He had carefully worked out what he wanted to say and cited facts and figures to support his argument.

His proposal differed from George's in a number of essential ways. Davitt proposed state confiscation of the land, with compensation paid to the landlords, whereas in Georgian theory the landlords had no right to the land, hence there was no obligation to compensate them. Davitt's projected single tax on land was to be based on an estimate of the costs of administering the Irish state, rather than on the value of rents—the unearned increment in Georgian analysis. But George thought the Davitt program his in principle, and he was jubilant. "At last the banner of principle is flung to the breeze," he wrote Ford. "What we have been praying for and quietly fighting for is so far accomplished."[8]

Thus midway through 1882—the long-anticipated year—the New Departure was in trouble. The Kilmainham Pact, whose broad outlines were now apparent to the public, distressed the extreme nationalists. Even more distressing was Davitt's new course of action. The Manchester and Liverpool speeches aroused intense interest on both sides of the Atlantic. The press interpreted them as a challenge to the Kilmainham arrangement and as efforts to widen the land war beyond the confines of Ireland. Davitt appeared to be abandoning nationalism for international social reform. John O'Leary, that inactive and incorruptible man, ticked off Davitt in this characteristic sentence:

> I and others have long since held that Mr. Davitt was not a nationalist at all in any sense intelligible to us; but only some sort of an internationalist and socialist, in some sense, not intelligible even to himself.

Davitt's endorsement by socialist and labor reformers in Britain and the United States appeared to substantiate O'Leary's wit.

Davitt's nationalism like that of Thomas Davis earlier was informed by a strong social conscience. At Liverpool, Davitt made it clear that he would prefer land nationalization to take place under an independent Irish government, but he also—to the dismay of O'Leary and others—declared that it could be accomplished satisfactorily under English rule: "Better to have the land of our country administered by even an Executive English authority," he said in his peculiar style, "than see it made the instrument of social slavery and degradation of tyranny and exaction by the merciless and polluted hand of Irish landlordism." The Land League had been an admirable mechanism for accommodating Davitt's social to his political interests. The Kilmainham agreement, however, forced him into the disagreeable position of either setting aside his land reform convictions, now fully matured, or of taking the chance of striking out on his own in the hope perhaps of dragging Parnell along. The initially unfavorable reaction to the Kilmainham *dé marche,* even in Parnellite ranks, may have persuaded Davitt that Parnell could be made to renew the land agitation.

Much depended on the United States, where Davitt was due to arrive on Sunday, June 18. Without Irish-American financial support the agitator could do little. And in the weeks before his arrival a strong tide was building up against him. His antagonists abroad (notably James J. O'Kelly, devoted Parnellite Member of Parliament and formerly of the New York *Herald*) kept the Atlantic cable hot with hostile reports that were carried throughout the United States by the Associated Press and appeared regularly in the New York *Herald* and the *Irish Nation.* The *Irish World* was a powerful ally, but its influence was fast running out. The Cleveland scandal, in which Bishop Gilmour and the Ladies Land League were still at odds, suggested the imprudence of going on with so divisive an agitation. Land League contributions to the *Irish World* had dropped from $12,000 in February to $5,000 in April and were still falling off. The Boston *Pilot* expressed the American consensus on June 17 when it regretted that Davitt had turned from Irish nationalism to the pursuit of Utopia. "He does not know the American people or the Irish people if he believes they will follow him into such an uncertain enterprise as the entire abolition of ownership in land."

The reception given Davitt when the *Germania* arrived in New York harbor was fully as tumultuous and discordant as that accorded the *Cuba* Five a decade earlier. About two hundred *Irish World* partisans went down the Bay to cheer his arrival, but at the Everett Hotel he was besieged by hostile interrogators. Their animus had been fed by that morning's *Herald,* which reported Parnell's dissatisfaction with Davitt's activities. The hero of the land agitation was forced on to the defensive.

In his first public appearance on June 19 at the New York Academy of Music, Davitt tried hard to find a middle ground between laying down a specific challenge to Parnell and knuckling under to him. In a speech in which humility and belligerency alternated, the former Fenian denied any desire on his part to take over the leadership, pointing out that his low social status precluded that possibility. Nevertheless, he asserted his right to speak out on the land question, for which he had suffered so much. He put forward land nationalization only as a possible theoretical solution in order to sound out public opinion. He concluded by asserting his loyalty to Parnell but only under certain ill-defined conditions. The hour demanded "fidelity to Parnell's leadership as long as Parnell remains true to Ireland and no longer."[9]

Thereafter, in a tour that took him to the Irish centers in the East and Middle West, Davitt step by step withdrew from the advanced position he had taken at Liverpool. At Boston he said, "I would sooner have my other arm severed than allow myself to be an obstruction to any plan laid down by Mr. Parnell. The nationalization scheme is my own and I do not urge its adoption or even its consideration." To the Irish of Albany, he announced that he would rather jump into the Hudson river than oppose his chief. By the time he had reached Chicago, Davitt had abandoned whatever hopes he had had of going on with the land agitation. Acting in accordance with his understanding of the New Departure, Devoy had helped Parnell to prevail.

Thereafter, Davitt moved out of the inner circle of the nationalist movement to create for himself the role of loyal opposition to Parnell. The Land Leaguer's greatest days were behind him, but he could take comfort in the realization that the agitation he had organized resulted in reducing the tenant farmers' rents by millions of dollars and preparing the way for their eventual takeover of the land they tilled.

Henry George and his disciples were angered by Davitt's performance. At Manchester, declared Louis F. Post's penny-daily, *Truth*, "Davitt had lifted the colors of the labor army; at Liverpool, he began to unfurl them; but before his first public appearance in America . . . he had packed them away and swung out a little green flag with a harp on it."[10]

The green flag with its harp stood for many things that were meaningless to Henry George. It evoked that saga of suffering that was so deeply imbedded in the Irish mind that it could hardly comprehend the sufferings and injustices borne by others. The flag and the harp stood for nationality, that transatlantic solidarity which promised to win for the Irish the world's respect. Davitt and George were asking the Irish to commit themselves to the untried, to that not sanctioned by American opinion. They wanted respect and they feared ridicule. "We do not wish to see the Irish national leaders donning the rusty armor of Don Quixote to make their country the laughing stock of the world," said John Finerty, who otherwise was prepared to play the clown in ways habitually approved by Americans.

Davitt's rejection by the American Irish was not, of course, unanimous. Patrick Ford and his followers remained loyal. Father Edward McGlynn, pastor of St. Stephen's Roman Catholic Church, became a convert to land nationalization and at Davitt's reception in the New York Academy of Music eloquently urged Davitt to stand up to his antagonists. Another convert was Terence V. Powderly, Grand Master Workman of the Knights of Labor and a Clan na Gael member, and the Irish-dominated districts of the Knights were strongly for Davitt and George. Also committed was the Central Labor Union of New York City, which was first organized at the great Cooper Union rally on January 30, 1882, in support of the No Rent Manifesto. The impulse for social reform that arose out of the 1870's was far from spent. Nationalism triumphed in 1882, but four years later the humanitarian reformers would once again challenge Irish conservatism.

Parnell was the chief beneficiary of Davitt's gamble in 1882. Had Davitt not challenged him the Home Rule leader would almost certainly have found himself in trouble with Irish-America. The Kilmainham Pact brought the Irish movement on to a course far from that contemplated in the New Departure. But Davitt's thrust to the left gave the American extremists no choice but to support Parnell. These events appear to have made them more determined than ever to build up their own block of power in the United States that would make them a force to be reckoned with in Irish affairs. The committee of seven, established at the Chicago convention, having come to nothing, the Clan na Gael leaders joined with Davitt in Chicago to found a substitute—the Celtic Confederation. But this, too, proved abortive. Not until the American National League was founded in April, 1883, did they have an organization that came close to expressing their dreams.

The deal here in New York by which the Democratic majority was cut down . . . was one of those rascally tricks of the political machine that have as little relation to nationality as they have to religion or morality.

The Irish-American (New York),
December 20, 1884

We can get the men to vote as we want them to, except for Mayor. We can't move them there. They have got it into their heads to vote for George and there it sticks.

A Tammany Boss, New York Sun,
November 3, 1886

CHAPTER EIGHT

Yearning for Power

NOTHING strikes the historian of the American Irish so forcibly as their desire to wield power. As churchmen, nationalists, and politicians, they were possessed by the need to bend others to their will. Perhaps this was to be expected of a people whose homeland was subject to the world's greatest empire, and whose national symbol was a weeping woman and broken harp. When in 1882 the American Irish chose Parnell, the "uncrowned king," over Davitt, the Christian reformer, they made a choice in favor of power. No other contemporary figure so fittingly represented their aspirations as the charismatic Parnell.

Whatever were the psychological sources of the Irish-American drive for power, there is no doubt that politics was of crucial importance to their life in the United States. It was the scaling ladder they needed to climb up out of poverty. For the great majority of Irish immigrants had neither the skills that make farmers and mechanics nor the experience and habits that make businessmen. They lacked even that kitchen culture possessed by German, Italian, and other immigrants, which enabled the more ambitious members of these groups to lay the basis for a comfortable living by catering to the culinary needs of their countrymen. Like the American Negroes, the Irish were the unskilled of

Anglo-Saxon culture. Unlike the Negroes, they had a strong sense of family and group solidarity, reinforced by their Catholicism, and an old tradition of employing these traits in political activity. As far back as the 1820's Daniel O'Connell in the Catholic Association had taught the Irish how to use their numbers at the polling booth to advance their interests. Priest, landlord, and nationalist had each in his own way contributed to this education. In the United States the Irish early found a home in the Democratic party. It offered them patronage in return for votes and a means of defense against the assaults of anti-Irish nativists.

Irish-American politics was the politics of realism, free of the American liberal's moralizing and distrust of the uses of power. "Convictions, whatever they may be, are never nominated here," says Denis Moriarity in Paul Leicester Ford's *The Honorable Peter Sterling* (1897), which nicely suggested Irish values and liberal dislike for them. Irish-Americans, however, were not without their own sense of righteousness. They regarded success in winning public office as a vindication of their nationality and religion. Even the more unsavory aspects of their political activity did not diminish this sense of moral achievement. In their St. Patrick's Day parades they bore witness to this pride.

Parnell was the most spectacularly successful Irish politician of the 1880's. Presiding over the Home Rule party and the National League, he established control over Irish politics down to the local level—control so long and vainly sought by nationalists—and in 1885-86 held the balance of power in the House of Commons. Less showy but almost as impressive were the performances of those Irishmen throughout American cities who battled their way into the ruling councils of the Democratic party's urban organizations. Their success was reflected in the spate of middle-class magazine articles lamenting Irish control of "our cities." But the most striking development of the decade were the massive attacks upon the Democratic party made by other Irishmen, for the most part nationalists and nationalist-reformers. Anticipated in the 1870's, the revolt against the Democrats came to fruition in the presidential elections of 1884 and 1888 and in New York's mayoralty race of 1886. In these internecine struggles of Irish-American against Irish-American, the old alignments of the Land League were apparent. The conservatives, led by Patrick Collins, stood by the Democrats; the extreme nationalists, led by John Devoy and Alexander Sullivan, committed themselves to the Republicans. Nationalist reformers like Patrick Ford joined the Republicans in 1884 and 1888 and supported Henry George in his bid to become Mayor of New York in 1886.

In attacking the Democratic party the nationalists expressed both their desire for power and their revulsion for the processes by which it was ordinarily achieved, their desire for a place in the sun and the rebel temperament that alienated them from it. They wanted to exercise influence over the direction taken by Ireland and the United States, and yet the deals and compromises with which power was pursued in the American party system were uncongenial to them. A commitment to the Republicans offered a solution to their difficulties. Leading a revolt against the party that numbered a majority of their countrymen satisfied the rebel temperament, and at the same time it promised rich rewards. The unswerving loyalty of the Irish masses to the Democratic party was, in the judgment of nationalists, both a symbol and a cause of Irish inferiority. It demonstrated that they had the hearts of slaves and assured Democratic leaders that in the distribution of patronage and formulation of policies they need pay little heed to the Irish. Should the latter play a more manly and independent role in party politics, their services would be more highly rewarded and both parties would have a greater regard for the national interests of Ireland.

John Devoy and Alexander Sullivan may have had additional possibilities in mind. Parnell's unexpected Kilmainham agreement, which had caught them off guard, still rankled. With the founding of the Irish National League of the United States in April, 1883, the Clan na Gael nationalists seemed determined to build up a block of power that would match Parnell's. The new organization, according to Sullivan, its first president, stood "not for a party, not for a man, but for united exiled Ireland." It was, said John Devoy, Irish-America's long-sought-for government; henceforth Parnell could be expected to deal directly with it and not as in the past with wrangling divided factions.[1] At about the same time—again under Sullivan's leadership—the Clan na Gael secretly inaugurated a campaign of dynamite terrorism in Britain. In this most violent expression of the American–Irish desire for power, the nationalists had still another way of bringing their influence to bear on Irish politics. Perhaps the Irish-American Republican movement represented a third possibility.

The two major American parties were in unstable equilibrium. A relatively light shift of votes could mean the difference between victory and defeat. If the nationalists could persuade the Irish-American voter to abandon his allegiance to the Democrats, especially in the key city of New York, the Republicans would win. The nationalists might then hold the balance of political power in the United States as Parnell would hold it in Britain in 1885-86. Clan na Gael influence then would be immense on both sides of the Atlantic.

Ambitions so grandiose were not beyond the imaginations of these daring men, and, indeed, an enterprise of this exalted nature would have justified in their own eyes the descent into the bogs of American politics. In any case, whatever their particular motives, their strategy was to win power by pulling the Irish-American voter out of the Democratic party.

There were, however, serious flaws in the strategy. It was assumed that the ordinary Irish-American cast his ballot in response to the pull of nationalism and the leadership of the John Devoys. On the basis of this assumption, Republican party leaders supplied the nationalists with money to carry on their Irish-American Republican clubs, their torchlight parades, and to publish their propaganda proving that the Democrats were agents of England. The assumption failed to consider certain realities of Irish-American life.

Most important of all, immigrant leadership was highly differentiated. Cleric, politician, and nationalist competed for influence

over the Irish-American community. Each in his own sphere of
activity was a personage of consequence. Though barriers separating the three activities were not, of course, rigid, it was, nevertheless, not a simple matter to carry influence over from one to
another. When the newly arrived O'Donovan Rossa ran for State
Senator in New York in 1871 against Boss Tweed, the Tammany
Irish threw rotten eggs at him. Patrick Collins's troubles as Land
League president had been due in large measure to nationalist
contempt for him as a mere politician, and John Finerty's career
as a congressman was a short one because he ran afoul of Chicago Democratic machine politics.

Among cleric, politician, and nationalist, conflict was inevitable. It was less acute between priest and politician, both of whom
had roots in the local community and shared its interests, than
between nationalist and politician. The former was a man of
passion, not prudence; his heart was fixed on Ireland. Frustration
afflicted him, making of him a wayward and disturbing personage
within the immigrant community.

John Devoy, for example, threw a scare into New York's Democratic leaders when during the campaign of Perry Belmont for
Congress in 1882, he raked up an old story charging Perry's father
—the banker and formerly head of the Democratic National
Committee—with fraudulently mishandling funds destined for
the Dublin Fenians. Devoy was sued for libel and given a sixty-
day jail sentence. John Finerty's Chicago *Citizen* attributed the
court's decision to the "Anglo-mania which runs high among the
bastard British of the seaboard metropolis." But Devoy with
greater realism placed the blame upon the Democratic party.
After release from prison he dedicated himself to blocking Perry
Belmont's bid for re-election in 1884. "Are your ballots to be cast
for your worst interests," the *Irish Nation* questioned Belmont's
Irish-American constituents, "at the dictation of English agents
who despise you. . . ." Belmont, however, was re-elected, and
Devoy once again suffered humiliation.

The politician was difficult to beat at his own game. He stood at the center of a structure of loyalties and interests that bound together the Irish in their neighborhoods. He was the strutting hero of his bailiwick. By means of his patronage obscure men got jobs and bigger men got elected to office. James Bernard Cullen's *Story of the Irish in Boston* (1889) reveals the numerous Irish who from the 1870's onward were appointed as city lamplighters, clerks, appraisers, and auditors and others who won seats on the Boston Common Council and in the lower house of the state legislature. The consequences of this were apparent when in 1876 the Fenians made an all-out effort to oppose the election of Charles Francis Adams as governor of Massachusetts. That distinguished man had aroused Fenian enmity while serving as Minister to Great Britain from 1861 to 1868. Adams lost the election, but not the vote of the Boston Irish. That vote was held for him by the emergent Irish Democratic leaders, Michael Cunniff, Patrick Maguire, and Patrick Collins. Their successful efforts infuriated the nationalists. "It was the work of the party machine," one of them complained. "Every sharper who had a friend expecting office, every hanger-on who expected to get a dollar from a ward committee . . . all were called in."[2] Against these concretions of Irish-American life, the nationalist in 1876 could offer only hatred and the abstractions of nationalism.

In the presidential elections of 1884 and 1888, however, the Republican nationalists possessed a number of advantages absent from the campaign against Adams. They had control over a national organization—the Irish National League of the United States, whose activities attracted widespread public attention. Alexander Sullivan, the League's first president, lectured throughout the country in 1883–84 and became a familiar figure to the ordinary voter. Nationalists had the support of some of the most influential Irish-American newspapers: Devoy's *Irish Nation,* Finerty's Chicago *Citizen,* Ford's *Irish World,* and General Michael Kerwin's New York *Tablet.* In 1888, the New York *Freeman's Journal,* which had been taken over by the Ford family, and Edward Fitzwilliam's Boston *Sentinel* joined the crusade. Matt Quay, Republican party boss, sponsored the *Irish World* and the electioneering efforts of Alexander Sullivan. Though Devoy was short of money in 1884, he found an angel four years later in the person of Wharton Barker, a Pennsylvania Republican leader and antagonist of Quay within the party. Barker supplied Devoy with more than $35,000 to finance the Irish-American Anti-Cleveland and Protective League of New York.[3]

But the greatest advantage possessed by the Irish-American Republicans lay in the growing tensions generated within the Democratic party by the Irish Democrats' demands for more power. Every office won only whetted the Irish appetite for more, and they were full of complaints that they were not receiving their just deserts. On the other hand, among Democrats not of the Irish-American community, there was developing a powerful feeling of resentment against the Hibernians. Like the Negroes in the 1960's, the Irish in the 1880's were feeling the middle-class backlash.

William R. Grace felt this hostility acutely when in winning the race for Mayor of New York City in 1880—the first Irish Catholic to do so—he ran far behind the Democratic ticket. Both the New York *Herald* and the *Sun* had voiced their concern for the city's public school system should Grace become mayor. More troubling to the Irish was the refusal of American Protestants, both Republicans and Democrats, to grant Catholics the right of freedom of worship in state penal institutions. In New York between 1875 and 1885 dozens of Freedom of Worship bills were brought to the floor of the legislature, only to be killed out of fear of Protestant retaliation. Politicians who sponsored such bills were accused of truckling to Irish power.

Irish power was especially feared because it was tied so intimately to demagogic politicians like Ben Butler of Massachusetts and Carter Harrison of Chicago. Tammany Hall, of course, was symbolic for rural America of all the evils that had come over American life with the rise of the city.

The Civil Service reform movement, which gained momentum after a crazed office-seeker assassinated President Garfield in 1881, served to focus the resentments of Protestant America. The movement had no appeal for the Irish; in their view it was simply a device to shut them out of office. But the urban middle class— the readers of *Harper's*, the *Atlantic*, and Godkin's *Nation*—took up the cause as though it were a new religion. They found their white knight early in the 1880's in the person of Grover Cleveland.

As Mayor of Buffalo and then from 1882 to 1884, as Governor of New York, Cleveland made his name as a stern Democrat and a conspicuous protector of the public purse. Having created a strong political organization upstate, he shrewdly entered into direct conflict with Honest John Kelly of Tammany Hall and won every time. He blocked the nomination of Thomas F. O'Grady, a Tammany Hall orator, for the New York State Senate, and that of William Purcell, Irish-Catholic editor of the Rochester *Union and Advertiser*, for Secretary of State on the grounds that they were Spoilsmen. At the Democratic national convention held in Chicago in the summer of 1884, the Cleveland forces and Tammany Hall engaged in a bitter battle. Kelly, O'Grady, and Purcell howled that Cleveland was anti-Irish and anti-Catholic. In reply, General Edward Stuyvesant Bragg of Wisconsin gave pithy expression to rural and middle-class antipathies when he said of the rotund Cleveland, "We love him for the enemies he has made."

Given the crucial importance of politics for the aspiring Irish, it is not surprising that they were alarmed by these events. Bragg's speech was regarded as heralding a revival of Know Nothingism. Other developments appeared equally ominous. A number of Orange Lodges and branches of the American Protestant Association, a relic of Know Nothing days, endorsed the former Mayor of Buffalo. After the Republicans nominated James G. Blaine, reputedly a Spoilsman and touted as a friend of Catholics, a number of upper-class Republicans of impeccable respectability bolted their party. The usually sound Springfield *Republican* announced that in Blaine's nomination it saw the "Pope's toe moving toward the presidential mahogony." The ethnic and religious antagonisms of the 1850's appeared to be re-emerging within the Democratic party.

It was this situation that gave Sullivan, Ford, Devoy, and the other Republican nationalists their opportunity. Sullivan was present at the Democratic convention in Chicago and there, along with Ben Butler, he raised the cry that Cleveland was an anti-Catholic bigot and an enemy of labor who had vetoed legislation helpful to the Irish working classes in New York. Subsequently, Butler joined the presidential race as the nominee of the almost fossilized Greenback and Anti-Monopoly parties with the obvious purpose of taking votes away from Cleveland. The Irish National League officially remained aloof from the struggle. Sullivan had resigned the presidency before taking up the campaign trail, but his successor, Patrick Egan, the former Land League treasurer who had fled to the United States in 1883, very early in the race came out for Blaine.

In the November election returns it was apparent that a significant number of Irish-Americans had turned against Cleveland. In New York and Boston his vote in the Irish wards was down about 7 percentage points below that which the Democratic presidential candidate, General Winfield Scott Hancock, had received in 1880. The Irish loss was offset, however, by the number of Republicans who voted for Cleveland, and he won New York State's electoral votes and therefore the presidency by a narrow margin. In the judgment of many contemporaries the election turned on the sensibilities of the Irish. According to this view, Hibernian voters were moving out of the Democratic party in massive numbers when an aging Presbyterian clergyman, the Reverend Samuel Burchard, shortly before the election, described it as the party of "Rum, Romanism, and Rebellion." This expression of a hoary Republican prejudice against the Irish and their Church—made in the presence of Blaine and quickly seized upon by Democratic propagandists—is thought to have checked the Hibernian swing to Republicanism and accounted for Blaine's defeat.

Though disappointed, the nationalists looked forward to 1888.

That year the Democratic party once again chose Cleveland and the Republican party turned to Benjamin Harrison, a lackluster Indianian with whom respectable Republicans felt at home. Once again the Irish-American voter occupied the center of the stage, and once again the campaign was enlivened by religious and ethnic animosities. The old charges of bigotry and of hostility to labor were leveled against Cleveland, and the Democrats recalled (or said they did) the occasion when Harrison said the Irish were fit only to dig ditches. Each side accused the other of sponsoring certain clauses in the extradition treaty with Britain then under consideration that would have made Irish terrorists liable to extradition.

But the Republicans had the most telling issue—from an Irish-American point of view—in Cleveland's advocacy of a substantial downward revision of American tariffs. Virtually all Irish-American leaders supported a high tariff policy as a protection against flooding the United States with British goods. Devoy's Irish-American Anti-Cleveland and Protective League of New York and the Anti-Free Trade League in which Sullivan, Egan, and Ford were active were designed to drive home the point that Cleveland's policies would enrich Englishmen at the expense of American labor. The Republicans also had a useful issue—especially among New Englanders—in the Bayard-Chamberlain fisheries treaty which Republicans charged sold out American fishing interests to the Canadians. When Cleveland sent the Treaty to the Senate for approval, Democrats found it expedient to ignore the President's advice and join with Republicans in defeating the treaty.

As if in confirmation of the Republican accusation that Cleveland was little more than an English agent, Lord Sackville, the British Minister to Washington, wrote that now famous letter asserting in effect that Britain would be pleased were Cleveland to be re-elected. Like Burchard's blunder in 1884, Sackville's in 1888 is presumed by historians to have significantly influenced the Irish-American voter and the outcome of the election. This time it was the Republicans who took New York's electoral vote, and Harrison who went on to the presidency.

Among the number of Irish-Americans rewarded for their efforts in behalf of Harrison was Patrick Egan, who was appointed Minister to Chile. Though he had good reason to be pleased, having been a United States resident for only a little more than five years, this and other appointments fell short of the great expectations entertained by the nationalists. They had been talking of Cabinet appointments. Probably, however, the rewards were not disproportionate to nationalist influence upon these campaigns. Certainly the Devoys and Sullivans had not been able to beat the politician at his own game.

National and religious feeling entered into these campaigns but do not appear of themselves to have determined their intricate patterns. In Chicago in 1884, the same Democratic politicians who turned a deaf ear to Cleveland worked to defeat John Finerty, the ultra-nationalist who stood for re-election to Congress as an independent. In New York in that same year the Democrats returned Perry Belmont to Congress, despite the frenetic opposition of Devoy. But the central fact is that Cleveland's share of the Irish vote in New York and Massachusetts was greater in 1888, when it is presumed Lord Sackville's stupidity turned the Irish against him, than in 1884, when Burchard's blunder is thought to have won him Irish votes. Very likely neither of these celebrated events had much effect on the outcome of the campaigns.

Patronage appears to have been at the heart of the matter. Cleveland's attitude toward the Irish while Governor, and his alleged advice in 1884 not to "overload the ticket with Irish," cost him votes in that year. Given the realities of presidential politics, however, he could not hope to win re-election and at the same time completely ignore the claims of the urban Irish political organizations. William C. Whitney, the Secretary of the Navy, was especially mindful of the need to deal with the Irish. The number of offices given to Irishmen in Rhode Island convinced one observer that they "hastened the prospects of wiping out forever the odious and un-republican distinctions made in this state between native and naturalized citizens." Elsewhere, however, the wounds were not so easily healed.

Patrick Collins was the key figure in Massachusetts. During the 1884 campaign he had been active throughout the East in behalf of Cleveland, checking the thrusts of Butler and the Republican nationalists, and he hoped victory would bring him high honors. John Boyle O'Reilly, who had also campaigned for Cleveland, thought a Cabinet post for Collins would represent a marvelous expression of confidence in the "Irish race." But the appointment was not forthcoming; and to add to Collins' sense of injury, the new President did not follow his advice in filling important patronage positions in Massachusetts. However much Collins may have been inclined to break with the Administration, he was in no position to do so. The Massachusetts Irish were not yet strong enough to go it alone without the help of the reform Democrats to whom Cleveland was listening. Moreover, there was some justice in Cleveland's position that perhaps Collins could recognize. Despite his efforts in 1884, he had not been able to stop the Butler organization, which retained some vestige of its once great influence, from substantially reducing the Irish Democratic majorities in Massachusetts. Collins swallowed his pride, worked for the Administration, and waited for better days.

With Butler out of the way in 1888, the Boston Democrats won back the votes they had lost to him four years earlier. Cleveland took 80 per cent of the vote in Boston's most heavily Irish wards, surpassing Hancock's percentage in 1880 and approaching that of Butler when that magnetic man rolled up his record Democratic vote in the 1883 gubernatorial race.[4]

In New York, however, the Irish occupied a stronger position and played a more independent game. With the help of Whitney, Cleveland's relations with Tammany improved following the death in 1886 of Honest John Kelly and his replacement by Richard Croker. In the interest of blocking the presidential ambitions of New York's Governor David Hill—a shrewd and popular Democrat—the Administration released patronage to Tammany. In 1888 Cleveland ran somewhat stronger in the Irish Assembly Districts of lower and midtown Manhattan than he had four years earlier, but nevertheless he ran far behind David Hill. Tammany was more interested in municipal and state offices than in the presidency and probably traded presidential votes for Republican support of Hill and Hugh Grant, Tammany's victorious candidate for Mayor. "Johnny" O'Brien, Republican leader of the 8th Assembly District, was notorious for arranging such deals.[5]

In any case, the issues raised by the nationalists and accidentally interjected into the campaigns by Burchard and Lord Sackville appear not to have been immediately relevant to this power struggle. As the forthright editor of the *Irish-American* said: "The deal here in New York by which the Democratic majority was cut down . . . was one of those rascally tricks of the political machine that have as little relation to nationality as they have to religion or morality." He was writing of 1884, but his words apply equally as well to 1888. Nationalists could and did exploit the conflicts within the Democratic party, but they remained conflicts within the party, subject to decisions by the party leaders. In Brooklyn, where Hugh McLaughlin was boss, Cleveland got a high percentage of the Irish vote in both campaigns, running in 1888 only a step behind Governor Hill.[6] McLaughlin had no love for Tammany and little reason to quarrel with Cleveland.

To say that patronage questions were the essential matters in these campaigns does not mean that the Irish were mere job seekers or were indifferent to the ethnic and religious emotions which nationalist propaganda sought to arouse. But the issues on which nationalists focused, such as the tariff and the extradition treaty, were complex and abstract, remote from the immediate concerns of the ordinary Irish voter. Moreover, whatever emotional appeal they had was blunted in the course of the campaigns. Every Republican charge was met by a Democratic countercharge, so accusations canceled each other out. If the Irish and other patriots were alienated by Cleveland's initial stand on the fisheries question, they could take comfort in his later vigorous assertion of American rights on the matter. If Lord Sackville was an embarrassment, his rapid recall in response to Cleveland's demand was an asset. And needless to say, neither of the Republican presidential candidates in these campaigns was an Al Smith or John F. Kennedy, capable of arousing deep-felt ancestral loyalties.

Loyalties of this nature were bound up in the ward political organizations. Though today we are prone to romanticize the boss system, forgetting its dishonesties and brutalities, it is nevertheless true that it gave the poor a stake in American society when they badly needed it. The anarchy of the Molly Maguires in the Pennsylvania hills is suggestive of what might have taken place in the emerging American cities had there been no Irish Democratic political organizations. They gave the Irish access to jobs and power. Along with the Church and the labor movement they held the key to the Irish future. Although the ward boss was a more ambivalent figure than the revolutionary martyr, he too was a champion of the people. The promises of American life were bound up in him and his organization. That is why a quarrel with the Irish over patronage could take on the character of a holy war.

Irish-American political organizations, of course, did not fully meet the immigrant community needs. The politician was too immersed in the day-to-day work of winning power within the American social structure to formulate programs that would alter the structure in favor of the disadvantaged. The politician was a conservative who dealt with what is rather than what might be. Irish working-class discontent, mounting ominously in the 1880's, found no adequate outlet in the urban Democratic machines. When this discontent came to a boil in 1886, it generated independent labor challenges to the major parties in a number of American cities. The most important occurred in New York City, where labor's champion was Henry George. Four years after the spring of 1882, when the American Irish had let him down, the

San Francisco land reformer was again riding a powerful tide of unrest.

In the winter and spring of 1886, tens of thousands of workers throughout the country had downed tools and gone out into the streets. Strikes, lockouts, and boycotts (a name and technique borrowed from the Land League) shook the nation with violence. In Chicago on the evening of May 4 a bomb was thrown at a workers' mass meeting, killing six policemen. Following the Haymarket Massacre a wave of anti-labor hostility swept over the nation. In New York in July six trade-unionists were sentenced to prison for carrying on a boycott of a German-American beer hall. This decision climaxed years of frustration and drove the Central Labor Union—first organized at a Cooper Union rally in support of the No Rent Manifesto—into politics. The United Labor party (U.L.P.) was founded with John McMackin, former Fenian and labor leader as party chairman, and Henry George as its candidate for Mayor of New York in the forthcoming elections.

Thousands of New Yorkers of the most diverse persuasions rallied in support of the U.L.P.: Irish and Germans, socialists and greenbackers, skilled and unskilled workers. Also attracted were many Irish political adventurers who for a decade or more had been associated with various movements to break Tammany Hall.

Irish support for George may also have been influenced by events abroad. In June, 1886, the House of Commons rejected the Liberal party's Home Rule Bill, which would have given Ireland a measure of self-government. In the following month, the Liberals brought the issue to the British people in a general election and were defeated and turned out of office. The Bill, which represented Parnell's greatest triumph, had aroused great hopes in the United States. The defeat hurt. Dynamite terrorists, who had been quiet for a year or more out of deference to Parnell, were once again heard to mutter about the need for dynamite. Perhaps George helped the American Irish to express a deep sense of frustration. Far more than Blaine, two years earlier, or Harrison, two years later, he was capable of triggering off Irish emotion. In 1882 he had championed Michael Davitt and the

Irish underdog against the conservative nationalists and clerics; now he was again championing the Irish underdog, and again the conservative nationalists and clerics opposed him. Patrick Ford and Terence V. Powderly, who had stood with him in 1882, were with him in 1886; so was Father Edward McGlynn, the St. Stephen's priest beloved by the poor Irish. Powderly and Ford, who had been Blaine Republicans two years earlier, toured the tenements with George in 1886, seeking support for the reformer.

The campaign released long-repressed energies. The hitherto hostile Irish-Americans and German-Americans linked arms fraternally in that unusually warm autumn as they listened to the prophet from San Francisco. At Cooper Union and Chickering Hall, at Jones Woods and Sulzers Harlem River Park, George spoke in his moving way of the slum tenements and man's inalienable right to land, of poverty and suffering that could be wiped out were man to do God's will.

The voting on election day shocked the politicians. "We can get the men to vote as we want them to, except for Mayor. We can't move them there. They have got it into their heads to vote for George and there it sticks." So complained a puzzled Tammanyite. Running against a united Democratic party—a rarity in those years—George polled over 67,000 votes in the city and averaged close to 34 per cent of the total vote cast in the lower and midtown Assembly Districts where the Irish were strong.

More than half a century later, the great campaign of 1886 would be remembered by many who as children had marched with their parents in the parades for Henry George. More often than not their memories were overlaid with bitterness. For that crusade split the Irish-American community wide open, revealing an anti-clericalism that had been festering since the 1870's and a dislike for the heavy hand of episcopal authority that reminds one of D'Arcy McGee's battles with Archbishop Hughes. During the course of the campaign, Father McGlynn had been suspended by his superior, Michael A. Corrigan, the Archbishop of New York, for speaking out in George's behalf. And shortly before the elections the archdiocesan chancery office had turned over to a spokesman for Tammany the Archbishop's critical views of George's theories. Like Bishop Gilmour of Cleveland, Corrigan encouraged the poor to accept their lot with Christian resignation. In July of the following year, McGlynn was excommunicated for refusing to obey a summons from Rome to state his side of the story. There was within this priest, born in New York of Donegal immigrant parentage and educated in the city's public schools, a strong streak of old-fashioned American evangelicalism. Episcopal pressure only persuaded him to take more vigorous action in support of George and the social gospel. Behind him he had many of his old St. Stephen parishioners and many thousands of Irish Catholics throughout the nation. In the month before his excommunication a massive parade in his honor moved down Broadway to Union Square chanting, "Don't go to Rome."

Father McGlynn's troubles were a chapter in a larger story of U.L.P. disintegration in 1887. Backsliding inevitably followed upon the intense, near-religious excitement of 1886, and within this highly heterogeneous party, old ethnic, religious, and ideological antagonisms soon reasserted themselves. Unlike the major parties, which, of course, suffered from similar strains, the possibilities of public office and patronage were too remote (and for many of these idealists, of secondary importance) to act as a restraint upon faction fighting. Pressure from the Archbishop exerted on the party a pull to the right, while the affiliated Socialist Labor party was a force pulling to the left. George, McGlynn, and McMackin appear to have been groping, almost instinctively, toward a middle ground. They found it in an affirmation of a traditional Americanism which distinguished them from Roman authoritarianism, on the one hand, and German socialism, on the other.

In short, George and his followers in 1887 sounded suspiciously like Know Nothings. Though the land reformer insisted upon the importance of the distinction between the legitimate and the illegitimate claims of the Church, it was a difference difficult to maintain in the heat of the controversy and was in any case not very meaningful to most Irishmen who had been trained to act reflexively whenever the Church was under attack. (Some Irish anticlericals, however, took the opportunity to even scores with the Church by raking up old papal scandals.)

It was not long before George's Irish support began to break down. Powderly withdrew his allegiance shortly after the 1886 elections, at a time when the Knights of Labor had reason to fear papal condemnation of their activities. Patrick Ford gave up the fight in October 1887 in the midst of the second U.L.P. campaign, when George was running for Secretary of State. Ford's withdrawal was accompanied by a long statement explaining why, as a Catholic, he could no longer support McGlynn and George. The statement was widely circulated and perhaps contributed to the San Francisco reformer's smashing defeat in 1887. In New York City he obtained only 37,000 votes, 9,125 of them cast in the strong Tammany districts of lower and midtown Manhattan, where he received a surprisingly high 22 per cent of the vote. In the following months the inevitable dissolution of the crusade continued. McGlynn and George quarreled, the latter throwing his support to Cleveland in 1888 on the basis of the tariff question. McGlynn continued the fight against Tammany and its allies in the diocesan chancery office. But the crusade was over. In the 1888 elections the labor vote dropped to insignificance, and Tammany emerged stronger than at any time since the dissolution of the Tweed Ring in the early 1870's.

The campaign of 1886 and its turbulent aftermath had a number of consequences. It demonstrated to a later generation of ecclesiastics the imprudence of Archbishop Corrigan's effort to dam up a flood of social unrest with a doctrinal formula. It convinced the leaders of labor that bread-and-butter unionism was preferable to following idealists into the bogs of politics. Similarly, it persuaded many an Irishman that bread-and-butter politics—the politics of patronage and power—was better adapted to Irish needs than the pursuit of utopia. As John Boyle O'Reilly surveyed the division between cleric and anti-cleric in New York's Irish community from the vantage point of Boston, he was dismayed. He took back the words of praise he had been heaping upon George and declared that a reformer's job was to talk, not act.

Furthermore, by attempting to build up a power base that would make their influence felt in American and Irish politics, the nationalists all but wrecked the National League in the United States. John Devoy's politicking in 1884 led in the following year to the financial collapse of the *Irish Nation* and to savage enmity between Devoy and Sullivan, whom the former blamed for many of his financial troubles.

Irish-American assaults upon the Democratic party, however, were not without value. There was point to the argument that Irish Democratic loyalties had been taken for granted and so were insufficiently rewarded. The possibility of a substantial Irish defection from the party no doubt in the long run gave them greater leverage in opening doors hitherto closed to them. In addition, Democratic politicians were forced to pay greater attention to the nationalist sensibilities of their constituents. Tammany Hall leaders after 1884 became increasingly active in the Home Rule movement, especially so after Henry George startled them in 1886. They became a major source of funds for Parnell, and they supported John Devoy's efforts to break Alexander Sullivan's influence over the National League. In this way Tammany Hall emerged from the tide rips of these years stronger than ever, the most compelling symbol of Irish-American power.

It is perhaps not too fanciful to conclude that the Irish-American politician was the heir of Daniel O'Connell, the realist who once said that an independent man was a man you couldn't depend upon; while the nationalist was an heir of Thomas Davis, who projected for the Irish people a legend of heroic, if remote, dreams. The nationalist shared with the politician a desire for power, yet the manipulation of power was not his function within the Irish-American community. He stood for the traditions of the Irish rebel, who placed justice above power. Although nationalist societies were inevitably pulled into American politics, they were meant to be transcendental, to soar above the realities of American life and fix the Irish consciousness on the glittering ideal of nationality.

'Twas Irish humor wet and dry
Flung quicklime into Parnell's eye.

JAMES JOYCE

I claim not to have controlled events, but confess plainly that events have controlled me.

ABRAHAM LINCOLN

CHAPTER NINE

A Handful of Dust

THE leaders of Irish-America were men of boldness and vigor. In the National League they drew together tens of thousands of Irishmen in a common enterprise that spanned the North American continent and brought to the attention of Americans in every major city the aspirations of Ireland. They were responsible, directly or indirectly, for providing Parnell with hundreds of thousands of dollars. For a people so precariously placed in American society, it was a heroic undertaking, more impressive in its way than Parnell's work in Ireland. It made international figures of the Irish-American leaders, men to be reckoned with in the affairs of two nations. Yet by the end of the 1880's their dreams—or most of them—had turned to dust. Despite their energies and gifts of mind and imagination, they could no more preside over the fortunes of Irish-America than over an earthquake.

At the heart of nationalist difficulties lay a certain ambivalence. Heirs of generations of Irish rebels, who had sacrificed their lives and fortunes, for glittering dreams, the American Irish were at the same time worshipers of the bitch goddess success. The pursuit of profits and power, which Thomas Davis had deplored, was idealized in the American environment. Every step up the business and professional ladder, every political office won and honor received became a token of Catholic and Irish vitality. Archbishop Ireland thought it a responsibility of Catholics to become millionaires. These aspirations, however, were at war with the spirit of nationalism. The latter was above all a thing of passion. It fed on the fires of wounded pride; it cherished memories of the intransigent dead; it pursued absolute virtue and nourished bold designs. The tensions created by this ambivalence endured not only among but within individuals. Beneath the well-tailored Prince Albert of many a second- and even third-generation immigrant there was the fanatic heart.

In the 1880's these tensions tightened. In the interests of Parnell's bid for Home Rule it was necessary that the American Irish bear witness to the Irish capacity for responsible self-government. They had to appear as wise as owls and sober as judges—the good citizens of the New World. Many were pleased to play this role, especially the wealthier Irish who for the first time since the Civil War became prominent in the nationalist movement. But the role was not congenial to the fanatic heart. While Parnell was building up his political forces between 1883 and 1885, Clan na Gael terrorists were slipping over the Atlantic to carry out dynamite attacks upon the House of Commons, London Bridge, and other symbols of British power. Not until the British political crisis of 1885–86, when Home Rule appeared forthcoming, was the terrorism brought to a halt.

The dynamite campaign was a disaster. It infuriated the British, dismayed the Americans, and sullied the image of the Irish as a sober and responsible people. The Clan na Gael nationalists gave their support to terrorism as in these same years they gave it to the Republican party in order to make their power felt in a world full of frustration. The result of both was to shatter Irish-American organizations and to stimulate murderous hatreds among their members. Only Parnell kept the Irish-American movement from complete disintegration. He held them together as a magnet holds iron filings. When the long-concealed story of his relations with Kitty O'Shea was revealed in the O'Shea divorce case in 1890 the magnetism failed, and the Irish turned on each other.

Close to 1,200 Irishmen met at Philadelphia's Horticultural Hall on April 26, 1883, to found the Irish National League of America. The old Land League, subsequently merged with the new organization, was represented by 468 delegates; the Ancient Order of Hibernians, the Catholic Total Abstinence Union, the Irish Catholic Benevolent Union, and virtually all other Irish-American fraternal and uplift societies were represented. Delegates from Canada and Australia were present.

An institution competent to manage the affairs of Irish-America was established. National authority, to which state and municipal councils were subordinated, was vested in a president, vice-president, and federal council. The council's day-to-day work was turned over to an executive committee of seven. Control of funds was vested in a central treasury, and the keys to that important office were entrusted to the Reverend Charles O'Reilly, a Detroit Catholic priest.

The major objectives of the National League were to support Parnell in achieving self-government for Ireland; promote the development of Irish industry; injure British manufacturers by boycotting British goods; foster the Irish language and arts "which have always secured for the Celt success and renown in every country"; and destroy "those baneful animosities of province and creed [and] . . . keep alive the holy flame of Irish nationality."

The Clan na Gael, now dominated by Alexander Sullivan, adroitly managed the convention. On the motion of the Reverend Dr. George C. Betts, a Dublin-born Episcopalian clergyman from St. Louis, a young enthusiastic Catholic priest, from Chicago, Maurice J. Dorney, was chosen the convention's temporary chairman. Said Betts of Dorney to the great applause of the delegates, "I have given him my affection and I would give him my life." Both clerics were Clan na Gael men. Alexander Sullivan was elected president, and Dr. William B. Wallace, a tall, saturnine New York City physician and a Clan na Gael member, was instrumental in choosing the important executive committee of seven on which the Clan subsequently had a majority.

Nevertheless, the conservatives present were not unaware of the Clan's maneuvering and were not without their own resources. They were led by Father Thomas J. Conaty, a Worcester, Massachusetts, Catholic priest whose County Cavan parents had brought him to the Bay State in 1841 when he was only four. A tall and rugged six footer, total abstinence man, and future Bishop of Los Angeles, Conaty blocked proposals to dissolve the Land League until satisfactory assurances were received as to the National League's purposes. Not until Conaty gave his approval of Sullivan did the latter agree to accept the presidency of the new organization.[1]

Sullivan made an energetic president. To convince Americans that Ireland's troubles were their troubles, he embarked on a speaking tour that took him through fifteen states, wrote numerous articles for the press and for respected journals like the *North American Review*. He appeared before the platform committees of both major political parties and persuaded them to adopt planks calling for restrictions on the purchases of American lands by European speculators. Aimed chiefly at English investors in western lands, this proposal suggests how the once-radical fight against land monopoly suffered dilution in the National League.

He also was active in agitating against the admission of Irish paupers to the United States. Traditional nationalist hostility to subsidized emigration from Ireland had been intensified by a clause in the British Government's 1882 Arrears of Rent Act which provided for loans to Poor Guardians in order that they might unburden themselves of the poorest of their charges by financing their emigration. Irish-American journals joined with native American journals in protesting against the paupers who were swept into the United States with the great flood of 1882.

Dirty and destitute, they were an acute embarrassment to the second generation yearning for America's good opinion. Their embarrassment fostered some strange behavior. When Charlotte O'Brien, daughter of Smith O'Brien, the Forty-Eighter, proposed that the Charitable Irish Society aid her in founding a home for immigrant Irish girls, she was at first refused and denounced by the Irish-American press as a British agent.[2]

In accordance with a resolution adopted at the Philadelphia convention in April, 1883, Sullivan and a most respectable group of Irish-Americans visited President Arthur in June to persuade him to take action. Subsequently, immigration officials at Castle Garden under powers granted them by the Immigration Act of 1882 began to turn back poor emigrants who gave promise of becoming public charges. The children of the Great Famine had already begun to forget.

In spite of Sullivan's efforts and those of his successors to the presidency, the National League failed to realize the great expectations of its founders. It fulfilled more or less nobly its function of providing Parnell with money, but as the excitement over Home Rule in Ireland rose to great heights in 1885–86, it found that it was only one among many contributors to the success of Parnell. Moreover, it was never able to exercise the control over its membership which its pretensions as a government for Irish-America demanded.

When Sullivan retired as League president in August, 1884, to take up the presidential cause of James G. Blaine, League members were assured that the organization itself would not be involved in the campaign. But this was a fiction. Michael V. Gannon, the handsome lawyer who presided over the convention and served on the important executive committee of seven, stood as Democratic candidate for Attorney General in Iowa, and Patrick Egan, the former Land League treasurer, who had succeeded his friend Sullivan as president, announced in September his preference for Blaine and the Republican party.

Egan had been a United States resident only seven months

when he declared himself for Blaine, having abandoned Ireland after the Invincible arrests turned up evidence allegedly linking the Phoenix Park murders to Dublin Land League officials. He made his home in Nebraska, where he established a flour-milling business and speculated in real estate. By 1888, Egansville in Lincoln County, Nebraska, was advertising lots in the Irish-Catholic press. His pronouncement in favor of Blaine shocked even John Boyle O'Reilly, and less well-disciplined Irishmen were soon at one another's throats. The Nebraskan's tenure as president was marked by vicious attacks upon him from Democratic party stalwarts and from the Devoy faction of the Clan na Gael and by rejoinders from him in which he did not hesitate to call his detractors "traitors to Ireland"—a dangerous accusation, given the inflamed tempers of those years. Aided by Sullivan and the Clan na Gael majority which he bossed, Egan weathered the storm. At the Chicago League convention in August, 1886, he and Sullivan had sufficient control to elect Egan's Nebraska patron, John E. Fitzgerald of County Limerick origins, to the presidency. A wealthy Nebraska rancher, banker, and railroad builder—the unholy trinity of the old radical Land Leaguer's wrath—Fitzgerald was dismissed by the Devoyites and Democrats in a curious snobbery as an "illiterate millionaire." He would preside over the disintegration of the National League in America.

The troubles that afflicted the League on the national level were active also in the subordinate councils and in the affiliated societies. Meetings had been called in Indianapolis, St. Paul, Chicago, Des Moines, Buffalo, Boston, New York, and elsewhere following the Philadelphia convention to ratify the constitution and establish municipal councils whose responsibility it would be to direct the League's affairs within the cities. To strengthen municipal council control, the constitution was amended at Boston in 1884 by a provision directing all branches to submit their funds to the municipal treasurer who in turn would forward them to the national treasurer. Thereafter, the municipal councils became the focus of intense faction fighting. The New York City council was the premier prize.

In the interests of the Sullivan-Egan faction, Michael D. Gallagher, a hatchet-faced jeweler of County Sligo birth, gained the council presidency in 1885. He was one of the Democrats who had bolted for Blaine in 1884, riding a white horse at the head of a line of former Democrats in the great Blaine procession held in the city that fall. His enemies asserted that he had tried to trade on his influence by offering to return to the Democrats in exchange for a fat political appointment. In 1886, a coalition of Devoy clansmen and Tammany Hall Democrats got control of the presidency and used it to try and overthrow the western leaders in the Chicago convention of that year.

The League's failure to establish order within its ranks was inevitable. It lay between two power centers, American party politics on one side of the Atlantic and Parnellism on the other. Each was a magnetic force superior to the League's. Parnell exerted an enormous pull. In that aloof and mysterious man was embodied that nationalism which alone provided the immigrant Irish with a basis for unity. His was almost a mesmeric influence. Under his leadership the once-proud demand for a sovereign Ireland was reduced to a claim for local self-government, without diminishing the sense of excitement and daring of the demand.

In the general election of December, 1885, his highly efficient political machine won eighty-six seats, almost precisely the margin of the Liberal majority in the House of Commons. Without Irish support, Gladstone could not command the House. Parnell had accomplished in Great Britain what Alexander Sullivan dreamed of doing in the United States. In the first six months of 1886, the Irish Party held the balance of power. To preserve the British constitutional system of two-party rule which Parnell's power threatened, Gladstone on April 8 presented his historic Home Rule measure to the House. Ireland was to have a legislature of two houses which would have control over all affairs not specifically reserved for the imperial parliament. Among the important reserved powers were control over excise, trade, and customs. The defection from the Liberal Party of Lord Hartington and Joseph Chamberlain, the Birmingham radical, and seventy-seven other Liberals doomed the bill. It was defeated in the House on June 8 by thirty votes. Gladstone then brought his case to the British people and was again defeated. The Liberals won in Scotland and Wales, but were decisively defeated in England. Lord Salisbury formed a Tory government on July 21. Gladstone and Parnell remained locked in a Home Rule alliance.

To Irish-Americans, the bill's defeat was a hard blow. Nevertheless, they could take comfort in Parnell's accomplishment of winning the greatest living Englishman over to the Home Rule cause. Even the rejection of Gladstone by the ordinary English voter—that paragon of Democracy in whom so much faith had been placed—did not diminish the dignity which the Liberal leader had conferred upon the Irish movement. When in October, 1888, the actor and Celtophile, James O'Neill, baptized his third son—the famous playwright of the future—he named him Eugene Gladstone O'Neill, thereby honoring Ireland's last great Gaelic champion, Eoghan (Eugene) Ruadh O'Neill, and her new English champion, the ally of Parnell.

Some measure of the magnetic force exerted by this alliance may be taken from an examination of the American League's financial history. Despite Sullivan's energies, the League failed to grow during his tenure, probably because of the lack of stimulus from Ireland. Only 553 branches, representing perhaps 40,000 members, were officially recorded at the League's second convention held at Boston in August, 1884. This was six fewer branches than the Land League had when it lay dying in the previous year. In this first fifteen months of its existence, the new organization collected a little over $38,000. But of this amount only $24,372 represented dues forwarded from the branches. As the constitution called for annual dues of not less than one dollar for each individual member payable to the national treasurer, it is clear that, for many, membership in the organization was only nominal. The exciting force lay outside. As the Home Rule crisis emerged in 1885–86, League membership and finances improved substantially but the pattern remained. In the nearly seven years between April, 1883, and January, 1890, during which a peak membership estimated at 58,000 was reached, $635,873 was raised but of this, only $66,890 or a little more than 10 per cent was collected in the form of dues.[3]

Clearly, the League was not an Irish-American government but a propaganda and money-collecting agency. It was in funds and membership weaker than some of its affiliated societies. The glory days of the Irish Catholic Benevolent Union were long past, but in 1886 it had a treasury balance of nearly $186,000. The rapidly growing A.O.H. possessed nearly $1,500,000 in 1890 and had an enrollment of over 168,000. They, of course, were benevolent societies, engaged in providing benefits relevant to the conditions of American life. The very irrelevance of the National League made it the repository of Irish-American dreams, but also ensured its weakness in dealing with American and Irish political power.

The nearest thing to a collision between the American League and the Parnellites occurred after the Home Rule Bill's defeat. At that time the American reaction was of the greatest concern to the Home Rule Party. Perpetuation of the Liberal alliance, upon which success now depended, was in turn contingent upon the pursuit of moderate policies lest Gladstone's English supporters be alienated. The revival of Irish-American terrorism would place the alliance under intolerable burdens. An American extremist—perhaps Margaret Sullivan, the bright and aggressive wife of Alexander, or John F. Armstrong, an Augusta, Georgia, dry-goods merchant of County Sligo origins and member of the executive committee of seven—had been to see Parnell in London in the spring of 1886 and left him with the alarming impression that the American irreconcilables were out for blood. Parnell and his associates therefore looked forward anxiously to the convention scheduled to meet in Chicago on August 18, 1886. An able team of Parnellites led by William O'Brien, the nervously brilliant founder of *United Ireland,* was dispatched to Chicago. Accompanying them was Michael Davitt, who was supporting Home Rule and was a close friend of Patrick Egan and Alexander Sullivan. A special railroad car, by courtesy of Chauncey Depew of the New York Central, carried O'Brien and his associates from New York to Chicago.

In that spring and summer, the American nationalists probably felt a greater need for Parnell than he for them. They were in trouble. The American League was torn and almost paralyzed by faction fights. Throughout the spring and early summer, Alexander Sullivan's enemies in New York and Philadelphia, the ill-matched Devoyites and Tammany Hall men, were utilizing the receptive pages of the New York press to ceaselessly attack the Chicago leaders. Rumors abounded that Sullivan and Egan, having embezzled funds and betrayed the dynamiters, were plotting to break with Parnell. They were accused of lusting for seats in a future Republican cabinet. From Chicago came reports that the Triangle, as the Sullivan-dominated triumvirate which ran the Clan were known, had placed Dr. Patrick Henry Cronin, Sullivan's most remorseless Midwestern antagonist, under sentence of death for treason.

Intransigents like Rossa and Finerty wanted to turn to terrorism again, or said they did, but clearly there was no future in dynamite. The bombing program from 1883 to 1885 had brought twenty-seven Irishmen to British prisons and blasted the extreme nationalist movement to splinters. Furthermore, the Haymarket Massacres of May 4 had removed whatever romance remained in the popular view of dynamiters. The Chicago bomb made clear the difference, as Synge's Pegeen Mike would say later in another context, between "a galous story and a dirty deed." Bishop McQuaid of Rochester, ever alert to make a telling pronouncement, likened the Haymarket bomber to the men of the Clan na Gael and the I.R.B. No good Catholic, he said, could in conscience belong to either organization.

In the face of these troubles, the American nationalists probably looked to Parnell to save them from themselves. Parnellism was a success, having brought English liberalism onto the Irish side. And Parnell was a hero, the greatest since O'Connell, an uncrowned king, a myth in his own time. The mere presence of his lieutenants at Chicago was a vote of confidence in the American League leaders. To attack him was to reject all the hopes upon which the League rested.

After stepping off Chauncey Depew's special train in Chicago, William O'Brien and his fellow delegates confronted the troublesome Alexander Sullivan. After some tense talk, according to O'Brien's account, they persuaded the Chicagoan to abandon any thought of opposing the Parnellite program.[4] In the deliberations of the following days, Sullivan served as a check on the extremists.

Trouble first broke out at the traditional August 15 picnic which the Chicago leaders held as usual at Ogden's Grove (their opponents held one at West Driving Park, across the city). Long John Finerty, perhaps under the influence of picnic beer, infuriated Davitt, the guest of honor, by a rousing speech rejecting Home Rule. Replying with the elaborate irony of the front-line fighter, the land reformer said it was "very easy to establish an Irish nation 3,000 miles away from Ireland by patriotic speeches. I assure you that it is no easy task . . . to do so in dear old Ireland."

Finerty subsided, only to break forth again at the convention. Beneath massive pictures of Gladstone and Parnell which decorated Chicago's old Central Music Hall, the former Indian fighter announced that "if I had my way I would kill every Englishman that came to Ireland as tyrant or ruler." He took special exception to a resolution supported by Davitt which proposed not only to endorse Parnell but to thank Gladstone and the English, Welsh, and Scotch democracy as well. Sullivan then came forward to assure the delegates that what was good enough for Michael Davitt, whose empty sleeve eloquently testified to the purest patriotism, should be good enough for them.

The convention delegates were very conscious of the attention focused upon them by the English-speaking world and the need for dignified deportment. Aside from Finerty's outburst, which was fully reported in the British press to the consternation of Liberals, the convention conducted its affairs with commendable decorum. Parnell was approved, Gladstone thanked, and the English, Scotch, and Welsh democracy assured of Irish-American gratitude.[5]

Although National League officials were never in a position to exercise any real power, they gave every appearance of doing so. At executive meetings grave matters were discussed, and commands and exhortations of interest to presidents, prime ministers, senators, and diplomats went out across the nation. Messages to and from Parnell moved across the Atlantic. President Fitzgerald did not fail to remember the Gladstones on their wedding anniversary. Moreover, the illusion was widely accepted for reality, contributing thereby to the concern, already noted, for the Irish vote and the willingness to grant some of the prizes for which they yearned.

Leadership in the League conferred a certain nobility upon men like President Fitzgerald who had made their way by adding their halfpence to the pence. For those still making their way, the League was a means of bringing their names forward. For all, it offered a participation in Ireland's romantic rebel story. And for the Irish-American community at large, the National League testified to the new Irishman of America: sober, industrious, respectable. President Egan in his valedictory at Chicago struck the familiar note: The League has made "the cause of Ireland respectable and respected among Americans and through that means has helped largely to elevate our race upon this continent."

The Home Rule movement was immensely popular in the United States. Americans who had feared the radical implications of the Land League could take pleasure in supporting a heroic struggle which aimed at giving Ireland the kind of local autonomy held by American states. American idealism, battered and frustrated in the Gilded Age, forced to find a hero in Grover Cleveland, had in the Parnell cause—especially after Gladstone's commitment—a ready object for its affections. Americans professed to find in Gladstone's bill an American solution to Britain's imperial problem, one that reconciled the needs of imperial power with the Irish right of local self-government. From Portland, Maine, to San Francisco, mass meetings were held throughout 1885 and 1886 at which many persons distinguished in public life spoke in support of Home Rule. Vice-President Thomas A. Hendricks, the Indiana Democrat, at a "monster meeting" in Indianapolis on September 8, 1885, sponsored by the National League's Indiana council, spoke enthusiastically of winning for Ireland "what we Indianians enjoy." In Iowa, Rhode Island, Connecticut, New York, and Ohio resolutions by one or both houses of the legislatures endorsed the Parnellite demands.

In the minds of many of these American supporters of Home Rule, there was perhaps the hope that a solution to the Irish problem in Britain would ease ethnic and religious tensions in the United States. At a packed Boston rally, Leverett Saltonstall, grandfather of the present United States Senator from Massachusetts and Patrick Collins's blueblood rival for Democratic party patronage, prophesied that Home Rule "will have its influence on this side of the Atlantic . . . here our two races—the Irish and Anglo-Saxon—will amalgamate and form the great American race."[6]

This was a hope that would be voiced many times until the Irish Free State was established in 1921, and though it obviously ignored the American origins of American difficulties, it was, nevertheless, correct in focusing attention upon the international aspects of the Irish problem. English observers in the 1880's were fond of saying that the "Irish Question was mainly an Irish-American question," and Irish nationalists, of course, were convinced that the two were bound up together. The Home Rule debate was almost as much Anglo-American as Anglo-Irish. American historical experience appeared supremely relevant.

The opponents of Home Rule likened the movement to the Southern struggle for independence. Supporters, following the lead of two brilliant essays by Edwin Lawrence Godkin, argued that it was the Reconstruction period following the Civil War which was pertinent. Of Protestant Irish origins, molder of American middle-class opinion as editor of the *Nation* (named after Davis' paper) and the New York *Evening Post,* Godkin identified the Federal Government's failure to rule the South during Reconstruction, with all its Irish-like episodes of violence and disdain for law, with the British failure to rule Ireland through coercion. The South's return to a creative role in American life, symbolized by the Democratic party's 1884 victory, he thought indicative of what Ireland might do were she granted local self-government. From the point of view of American history, it is an interesting argument, suggestive of American liberal reasoning in abandoning the Southern Negro to white rule.[7]

The American Irish also figured largely in the debates. The rising and respectable Irish were pointed out by Gladstone's supporters as clear evidence that Ireland was capable of self-government; while the violence of the dynamiters and the corrupt ways of American Irish politicians were considered by the Unionists as sufficient evidence of the pessimistic view of the Irish character which generally prevailed in England. At the opening Home Rule debate in the House of Commons one of Gladstone's lieutenants, Sir William Harcourt, unwisely warned that the bill's rejection would bring the Irish wolf dog of vengeance across the Atlantic. At the debate's close Parnell assured the House that it was the promise of Home Rule which had quieted the fiery temper of Patrick Ford.

It is doubtful, however, that either the reputable or disreputable Irish-American influenced the House of Commons debate much one way or the other. The antagonists in a very human way no doubt saw what they wanted to see in the behavior of Irish-Americans. English contempt for the Irish—hardening with the rise of racist dogmas—was not likely to be significantly influenced by a handful of bourgeois Irish-Americans. Nor had Gladstone taken up Home Rule out of reverence for the redeemed

Irishman of North America. He was responding directly to the will of the Irish people who so overwhelmingly, outside of the Northeast, gave their votes to Parnell.

Nevertheless American and Irish-American financial support and their more intangible moral support were of incalculable aid to the movement. Gladstone was well aware of the difficulty of dealing with a powerful party, whose resources were drawn from outside Ireland. Should the Home Rulers backed by American opinion and money have withdrawn from Parliament in the spring of 1886 in accordance with the New Departure program of 1878, as Dublin rumor had it early in 1886, the British Government would have been in very great trouble indeed.

On the other hand, it seems very likely that the British working classes, in whom Michael Davitt placed so much faith, were to say the least not disposed by the Irish-American dynamite campaign—only recently ended—to love the Irish. Hard times in Britain since 1884 had soured working-class tempers, and traditionally in such crises the Irish served the function of scapegoats. In the elections of July, 1886, English workers voted decisively against Home Rule.

It is probable, also, that Irish-America contributed to that climate of fear and uncertainty in which the Home Rule debate was conducted. Even among those who followed Gladstone, there were fears that the Home Rule measure might mark the first step in the dissolution of the British Empire. The Parnellites gave unequivocal assurances that they would accept the bill as the final settlement of Anglo-Irish difficulties, and they urged Irish-Americans to give similar assurances. And dutifully the Americans endorsed the bill. John Devoy gave his word that "there will be no serious effort for separation. I should prefer an Irish republic but I prefer the happiness of my countrymen to any ideal form of government." Assurances from others, however, carried an undertone of regret. Alexander Sullivan spoke of a "first installment of justice."[8]

Irish-American opinion regretted especially that the proposed bill did not give Ireland authority to erect tariff barriers behind which industry might be developed. That Ireland had enormous coal reserves and great industrial potential which cried out for a tariff policy akin to America's was an article of faith among Irish-Americans. During the early stages of the Home Rule debate, 8,000 Philadelphians were reported to be engaged in boycotting British goods under the direction of the National League's municipal council. Anticipating the Marshall Plan, the National League's headquarters in Chicago proposed a program of Irish-American subsidies and technical assistance to develop Irish industries. Given the Irish-American reputation for extremism—a reputation previously fostered by the Parnellites for tactical reasons—it is no wonder that some British Liberals, for whom free trade was a sacred cow, feared that Irish-Americans would strive to drive the Home Rulers beyond the modest measure of self-government offered in the Home Rule bill.

One of the most remarkable developments of the 1880's was the emergence of wealthy Irish-Americans into places of leadership in support of Home Rule. It had long been a matter of lamentation among nationalists that they could not bring into their projects those whose wealth and connections made them in many ways more valuable allies than the immigrant poor. Even had the well-to-do Irish felt keenly the humiliations which charged immigrant nationalism, the obligations of respectability would have kept them away from nationalist enterprises which so often became matters of ridicule. They found a sufficient outlet for their charity in immigrant aid societies and for Irish sentiment at the dinners of organizations such as the Friendly Sons of St. Patrick, where they sang "The Minstrel Boy to the War Has Gone" and shared their lavish Irish hospitality with members of the Society of St. George and distinguished political figures. The members of these organizations identified themselves with Irish gentlemen of the past like Mathew Carey and Thomas Addis Emmet. Indeed, these bodies retained some flavor of that early nineteenth-century cosmopolitanism that was so hostile to ethnic and religious bigotry.

Patrick Ford in the 1870's sketched the rich Irishmen in this way:

> Mr. MacPractical, a hard-headed Irishman, who has a fair knowledge of men and things and prides himself as one of those who, starting out with nothing in life, has by shrewd management, fought his way to success. . . . He has turned the other side of fifty with silver lining in his hair, and has aldermanic proportions. He affects a certain dignity . . . has tenement houses.

Not until after the Land League agitation had ended and Parnell had started on his conservative course did the Mr. MacPracticals come to his aid. When in 1880 he had come begging they kept their distance and gave their famine relief money to organizations founded by his antagonists. Michael Davitt in the *Fall of Feudalism* tells us that he was refused when he solicited aid from John W. Mackay, the Irishman who struck it rich in Virginia City's Comstock Lode. Virginia City miners were among Davitt's most enthusiastic supporters but Mackay told him that he had little use for either the agrarian or the national movement. "It was all a waste of . . . energy and means."

There were, of course, important exceptions; most notably, John E. Fitzgerald, the "illiterate" millionaire who, as he said, preferred to be president of the National League than President of the United States. But on the whole it was not until after 1884 that upper-class Irish-Americans came forward to work publicly for Parnell. Perhaps the increasing respectability of the movement attracted them; perhaps increasing social mobility within the Irish-American community blurred class lines, reducing the old sense of isolation. In New York the emergence of men like Morgan J. O'Brien and Joseph J. O'Donoghue was related to the assaults upon Tammany by the Republican nationalists and Henry George. Both O'Brien, a native New Yorker who in 1887 was appointed City Corporation Counsel, and O'Donoghue, a wealthy coffee merchant, were Tammany leaders. By identifying themselves with the Home Rule movement they probably hoped to take the play away from the radicals.

It was the Home Rule party's critical need for electioneering funds that provided the occasion for the well-to-do Irish to come forward. Throughout 1884 Parnell had made appeals for funds to the American League leaders but without striking results. These orthodox nationalists were reluctant to spend money to send Irish politicians into the British Parliament. A Parliamentary Fund was established but, as of the Boston convention in August, 1884, it had raised only $5,000. Following the presidential campaign of that fall which led thousands of Irishmen to fall away from the League, Major John Byrne, a Cincinnati businessman who had served briefly and unhappily as a League vice-president, took the lead in proposing establishment of an independent fund to aid the Parnellites. He was frank in announcing that he hoped to attract support from those well-placed Irishmen who feared involvement in the League's turbulence. Thereupon he was sharply attacked for catering to the rich Irish at the expense of Irish-American solidarity under the League. Byrne's plan, or variations of it, was widely adopted in American cities during the exciting months of the Home Rule struggle from the fall of 1885 to the summer of 1886. Home Rule Clubs and Parliamentary Aid Associations organized by citizen's committees and supported by the press raised hundreds of thousands of dollars and forwarded it directly to the Irish League treasurer in Dublin.

Among the most energetic groups was the Hoffman House Committee of the Irish Parliamentary Fund Association. Under the leadership of Eugene Kelly, the multimillionaire president of the Emigrant Savings Bank, backed by men high in the councils of the New York City Democratic party and the Friendly Sons of St. Patrick, the Hoffman House Committee promised to send Parnell $100,000 within a month after its organization in late November, 1885. It fell short of this mark, but by the following August it had raised $150,000. Archbishop Corrigan gave his support to the fund, and Tammany Hall, whose Assembly Districts were canvassed under the direction of Joseph J. O'Donoghue, contributed $20,000. National League leaders complained to Parnell of these independents, but the Irish leader replied that he was grateful for aid from any and all sources.

The emergence of the rich Irish nicely met the needs of the Parnell-Gladstone entente. Not only did they provide hitherto-untapped sources of funds, but they also offered Home Rule propagandists an opportunity to counteract the Tory strategy of discrediting the movement by linking it solely to disaffected radicals and irresponsible terrorists. It was during the debate on a Tory coercion bill in the spring of 1887 that the London *Times* began publication of its famous series, "Parnellism and Crime," which alleged treasonable ties between the Clan na Gael and Parnell and sought to establish, by means of letters bearing his signature, that he sympathized with the Phoenix Park assassinations. During this same debate, Gladstone requested the New York *Sun*, which in the previous year had collected $30,000 for the cause, to furnish him with the names of representative American supporters of Home Rule. Members of the Hoffman House Committe figured prominently in the *Sun's* list.

If Parnell could take comfort from the actions of the Hoffman House Committee, so could the committee find rewards in his prudent conservatism. The Home Rule crisis of 1886 was attended by falling agricultural prices in Britain, with a consequent increase in tension between the Irish tenant farmers and their landlords. When the Conservative government in the early fall of 1886 rejected a Parnellite bill to roll back rents set under the Land Act of 1881, agrarian violence multiplied, especially in the Southwest of Ireland. To control this Whiteboyism, the Plan of Campaign was organized under the leadership of two National Leaguers, Timothy Harrington and William O'Brien. Tenant farmers on various selected estates were called upon to deposit their rents with trustees appointed by the Plan's leaders until the landlord in question agreed to a reasonable reduction of rent. Parnell himself remained apart from the agitation. Though Arthur Balfour, the young dandy with tiger claws who was in 1887 made Chief Secretary for Ireland, ruthlessly fought O'Brien and Harrington as though they were outriders of red revolution, and the Vatican in 1888 condemned the Plan as a violation of private property rights, it was in its purposes essentially conservative. There were no cries from these leaders to abolish rents and no schemes to nationalize the land. The agitation remained within the framework of the legislation of 1881.

This conservatism was welcome to those in the United States who were struggling to control the influence of Henry George and Father McGlynn. Unlike most Americans, for whom Ireland's poverty offered opportunities for smug comment on the iniquities of British rule, the followers of George were insistent that the Irish struggle was identical with the "irrepressible conflict between natural right and vested wrong" in which Americans were engaged. When in June, 1887, O'Brien came to New York, following a Canadian tour in which he had been mobbed by Orangemen, arrangements were made by New York's Central Labor Union to have him address an immense rally. Upon learning that the meeting planned to adopt resolutions endorsing Father McGlynn and land nationalization and that he would share the speaker's platform with alleged associates of Irish dynamiters, O'Brien refused to participate. He would rather, he said, "be cut into pound pieces."[9]

While speakers at Union Square denounced him as a front man for American rack-renters, O'Brien attended a banquet at the Hoffman House, a hangout for Democrats and sporting men, where he was a guest of the Hoffman House Committee. Eugene Kelly gave him a check for $25,000, and a toast to Gladstone was drunk. When he left for home on the following day the gallant 69th escorted him to the steamer *Adriatic*, along streets lined with cheering thousands.

The Home Rule propagandist's image of the Irish-American as

the good bourgeois of the New World was not without basis in fact, and it most certainly expressed Irish-American aspirations. Nevertheless, it ignored certain realities. The immigrant ships had brought peasant passions and the traditions of Irish physical violence with them to the United States, where they were stripped of the customary checks of family and parish. In America, they were adapted to the struggle for power. Ability to use one's fists, as the political careers of John Morrissey, Honest John Kelly, and Richard Croker testify, gave a man decisive advantages. The urbanity of Hoffman House Committee members was impressive, but it was based upon the securities of wealth and Democratic party strength in New York. Elsewhere, Irish-Americans were engaged in a rough-and-tumble struggle for power. Harrigan and Hart could make a good joke of it, Irish-American sentimentality could gloss it over, but it remained. Violence was as much a fact of Irish-American life in the cities as it was of American frontier life in the West. It was an act of murder which in 1889 shattered the Irish-American community, embarrassing those who wanted to live their lives behind the lace curtains of respectability.

Hatreds had long been festering within the Irish-American community. They were especially virulent in the ranks of the Clan na Gael, many of whose camps had broken with the Triangle after 1886 and looked to John Devoy for leadership. In June, 1888, the two factions met in Chicago and temporarily patched up their differences. By agreement the executive was expanded from three to nine and a new slate of officers was chosen. But the dissolution of the Triangle could not wipe out the suspicions and hostilities which the years since 1883 had aroused. The two factions dealt warily with one another, and the antagonists went about armed with revolvers. The explosion came after Henri Le Caron, the British agent and former confidant of the Clan inner circle, revealed himself before the Special Commission.

The Commission had been established late in 1888 to look into the year-old charges by the London *Times* that Parnell and his followers were linked to crime and treason. Parnell's counsel had little difficulty in proving that the *Times'* famous letters, allegedly connecting Parnell to the Phoenix Park murders, were forgeries perpetrated by a disaffected nationalist and adventurer, Richard Pigott, who shortly afterward (February 29, 1889) committed suicide in a Madrid hotel room. From this ordeal Parnell emerged a hero more fabulous than ever. But among American nationalists there was little reason for rejoicing. The startling revelation that Le Caron, the friend of Devoy, Sullivan, Egan, and others, was a spy and his testimony that other informers were active within Irish-American organizations sent a shock wave through national-ist ranks. In Chicago on May 4, 1889 (the anniversary of the Haymarket Massacre), Dr. Patrick Henry Cronin disappeared, and on May 22 his mutilated body was found in a sewer near the Lake.

The doctor appears to have been a man possessed by a death wish. Born in 1846 near Mallow, County Cork, he was brought to the United States when he was an infant. Restless, ambitious, and intelligent, he drifted to Missouri as a young man, studied medi-cine in St. Louis, and in 1882 moved to Chicago, where he set up a private practice. Possessing a good tenor voice and being highly gregarious (at one time or another, he was a member of eight fraternal societies), he was a well-known figure in Chicago's Irish-Catholic community. He was also Alexander Sullivan's most severe Chicago critic. From 1886 onward, he had been morbidly confiding to friends that he expected to meet a violent death.

The origins of his murder were traced by the prosecution to a Clan na Gael "trial" convened in September, 1888, in New York, and later in Buffalo, to hear the old charges against the Triangle of having misappropriated funds and neglected the families of missing dynamiters. When the trial committee—on which Cronin sat—failed to convict, he retained copies of the trial evidence and utilized them to make still more attacks upon Sullivan. According to the jury's findings, plans were thereupon laid in Clan na Gael Camp 20 to do away with Cronin. John F. Beggs, a prominent Irish Republican, Daniel Coughlin, a Chicago police officer and vassal of Alexander Sullivan, and two other members of Camp 20 were tried. Beggs was acquitted, Coughlin and two others were sentenced to life imprisonment.[10]

Cronin's funeral testifies to the American people's intense fascination with the Clan, whose secrets had been revealed by Le Caron in London and were now being further unveiled in Chicago. Like the Mafia today, the Clan was conceived to be wondrously powerful and mysteriously foreign. Some 12,000 people filed past the murdered man's bier in the 1st Cavalry Armory, and his funeral procession was the longest and most splendid Chicagoans had seen since Stephen A. Douglas died. At a citizens' protest meeting in Chicago's Central Music Hall, Robert Lindblom of the Chicago Board of Trade expressed American concerns, "We have come here to emphasize our rights as men and as American citizens and to protest against those rights being domineered by foreign influences and conspiracies."[11]

It is, nevertheless, clear that Cronin's murder was not a foreign conspiracy but a Chicago one which arose out of the tensions of Irish-American life. By his tireless efforts to publicize Sullivan's alleged wrongdoings, Cronin threatened the political influence of a powerful faction in Chicago politics. In the heavily charged atmosphere generated by Le Caron's testimony before the Special Commission, the rumors circulating that Cronin was an informer seemed highly plausible. Though Sullivan was briefly placed under arrest, there was no evidence to connect him with the crime, other than that those Irishmen tried were his liegemen. At the trial's proceedings, however, his name was repeatedly brought forward and his reputation was as much in the balance as the lives of the accused. That the stakes were high we may deduce from the effort made during the trial to bribe six of the jurors and from the presence of W. J. Hynes, a Clan na Gael enemy of Sullivan and Chicago's most famed trial lawyer, on the prosecution bench to which he had been "invited" by the State's Attorney. The effects of the murder were felt in Chicago politics for many years afterwards.

The murder and uproar which followed brought down the already stumbling American National League. For several years the League's executives had found it all but impossible to communicate with Parnell, and increasingly his envoys to the United States had appeared under auspices other than the League's. The development of alternative sources of American funds, Tory charges that he was the tool of American assassins, and then the Cronin murder apparently assured him of the wisdom of keeping his distance. As long as the League leaders remained his official representatives and paid deference to his leadership, they were able to maintain their hold over the organization. But when President Fitzgerald called for a convention in the spring of 1890 without first obtaining the permission of Parnell, the structure began to fall apart. Hugh McCaffrey, a Philadelphia file manufacturer, and Father McKenna, the Marlboro, Massachusetts, priest, resigned as first and second vice-presidents. In a statement carried by the Associated Press, the latter declared that he could no longer "associate with assassins or the tools of assassins." The League now was all but dead. John Boyle O'Reilly, who had himself but a few months to live, asked that the organization be allowed to die. Its chief purpose, he wrote, had been to create opinion in the United States favorable to the Irish cause; that objective attained, "the organization ceases to be useful, like the scaffolding around a completed building."

A few days before O'Reilly's editorial appeared, the Dublin leaders wrote on May 21, 1890, to Fitzgerald that they had come to the conclusion that the "influence of party politics in the United States of such a character as to render the existence of a centralized Irish national organization . . . undesirable."[12] Dillon requested the American leaders to relinquish control over funds gathered by the League in the United States. Reluctantly but dutifully, Fitzgerald complied.

Six months later the Gladstone-Parnell alliance was shattered by the scandal of the Parnell-O'Shea divorce case. Under pressure from his constituents, Gladstone asked Parnell to step down as Home Rule leader. Instead, he chose to stay on and make a fight against the "English wolves howling for my destruction." On December 6, 1890, a majority of the Home Rulers in Parliament repudiated Parnell's leadership. The Irish National Federation was organized as a rival to the National League, which the embattled Parnell still headed. In the brutal faction fighting which followed, the hopes of a decade were lost.

Throughout his career Parnell had invested an essentially prudent pursuit of power with the drama of Fenian heroics. That had been the substance of his charisma. But in the divorce crisis he chose to forgo prudence for a romantic defiance of his enemies. "A man having the destinies of a people in his hands," wrote a puzzled Irish bishop, "and bartering it away for the company of an old woman. . . ."[13] In this last struggle, Parnell embraced the myth he had created.

His fall was a hard blow to the American Irish. They had shared in his magnificence. In the crisis the extreme nationalists—Devoy, Finerty, even O'Donovan Rossa—rallied to Parnell. The conservatives of the Hoffman House Committee committed themselves to the National Federation and Gladstone. But most Irish-Americans adopted a position of disillusioned neutrality. "A plague on both your houses," announced the Boston *Pilot*. The nationalist dream had turned to dust.

The last convention of the Irish National League of the United States was held in Chicago on October 1, 1891, a few days before Parnell died of exhaustion in his Brighton, England, home. The sparsely attended gathering elected Michael V. Gannon, the handsome Davenport, Iowa, lawyer, to serve as the League's last president. In his address he called upon the Irish to stand together. "The enemies of our race are great and powerful. . . . Even here in this broad and free land we are the objects of their malice. . . . We are today the least organized nationality in America, while we have the most to contend with." The game, we may conclude, ended as it began, on a note of bitterness.

EPILOGUE

Hearts with one purpose alone
Through summer and winter seem
Enchanted to a stone
To trouble the living stream.

WILLIAM BUTLER YEATS

THE story told in these pages is a chapter in the Irish-American success story. In the decades of Parnell's leadership the achievements of the Irish were impressive. The peasant in Ireland was freed—or nearly so—from old tyrannies, and Home Rule was made a major issue of British politics. In the course of raising hundreds of thousands of dollars for the agitation in Ireland, the American Irish made themselves a force in American national life.

The year 1886 was decisive. Its exciting events—the Home Rule fight and Henry George's assault upon Tammany Hall—were the culminating episodes of tensions which had been building up since the Depression of 1873. Of the two forces thrown forward by the Depression—nationalism and the search for social justice—the former was the more powerful. The pull of nationalism brought into the Home Rule movement both radicals and conservatives, both the followers of Father McGlynn and the Hoffman House Committee, the extreme nationalists and the Catholic clergy. In this way, nationalism built a bridge across the gulf separating the rich from the poor. The priests active in the nationalist organizations contributed substantially to the American Catholic Church's efforts to hold on to the working classes.

Patrick Ford's Populism was especially consequential. His

178

monetary theories and, to a much lesser degree, his anti-Semitism anticipated Father Charles E. Coughlin, the Detroit radio priest and Sunday afternoon scourge of the New Deal. But Ford's efforts in behalf of the Land League and American labor unions place him in the forefront of those who have worked for social justice. The revolt of the Irish-American worker, which he and Henry George encouraged, forced thoughtful Catholics in responsible positions to a realization that the poor would no longer suffer the charity of the rich in an unjust society. Out of this realization would in time emerge new Catholic approaches to social problems. A major clerical figure in this development was Monsignor John A. Ryan, driving force behind the National Catholic Welfare Conference, antagonist of Coughlin, and friend of the New Deal. He came from a family of Minnesota Irish who subscribed to the *Irish World*.

Of the greatest consequence for the future was the development in the 1880's of Irish-Americans as a political force in the nation. Politics would remain their dominating passion. Out of their concentrated numbers, the techniques of organization learned from O'Connell, and a deep driving desire for power, they built the structure of modern urban politics. In this and the analogous work of providing leadership for the American Catholic Church they were at their most creative. But they would not build that city upon a hill that had been the dream of Thomas Davis and Henry George. Instead, they would become the great pragmatists of American politics. Means rather than ends would be their preoccupation. Power for its own sake and for its subsidiary benefits would give them satisfaction. When in 1886 and 1887 there developed a showdown between power, represented by the major parties, and ideals, represented by the United Labor party of New York, even the reformers like Patrick Ford and John Boyle O'Reilly chose power. Only slowly in the twentieth century would the ethical and social concerns for which O'Reilly and Ford had stood find some measure of welcome in Irish-American political organizations. Even so, as any Boston resident can testify today, the old Irish relish in the game for its own sake still survives.

Despite their successes, Irish-Americans would remain throughout much of the first half of the twentieth century an embittered people. The attitudes expressed by Gannon at the last National League convention would endure, sustained by the American Protective Association movement and later by the Ku Klux Klan. In part Irish-American bitterness was functional. A sense of suffering was the fuel which kept Irish-American organizations going. Nevertheless, so long an immersion in self-pity was bound to have unhappy consequences. The Irish wanted power, and they got it. But at a price.

For one thing they made themselves a national joke. In the 1880's, while busily chasing the Comic Irishman out of the theater and badgering politicians for this and that in the name of the suffering Irish, they were at the same time creating a new comic Irishman—the Professional Irishman. The joke had consequences, for the Irish had something to say to the nation in the early twentieth century, but few were willing to listen. The Irish voice was too easily discounted as mere Hibernianism. Finley Peter Dunne was able to break through the hostility and bring his ironies to a national audience but only by adopting the device of speaking through a Comic Irishman—"Mr. Dooley" of Archey Road, Chicago. The device had obvious limitations and, in any case, Dunne himself was soon absorbed into the Establishment.

Basic to Irish-American bitterness was the fact that their influence in public life increased out of all proportion to their status in private life. They could run the cities but could not get into the country clubs. The consequences of wielding power in a community whose social leaders did not accept them encouraged the Irish in their delight in power for its own sake, apart from the community's needs. Wherever social discrimination against the Irish was intense, political cynicism became a way of life.

Irish successes, therefore, tended to intensify their sense of isolation and the narcissism that flowed from it. The generosity of spirit which had animated O'Reilly, Ford, and others early in the 1880's diminished substantially after 1886. Organized Irish-American life became increasingly shrill. No one reflected this quite so sensitively as John Boyle O'Reilly. When in 1887, the British American Association was granted use of Faneuil Hall—Boston's symbol of liberty and free speech—to celebrate Queen Victoria's Jubilee, a loud roar went up from the Irish. "May my tongue cleave to my mouth if I ever speak a word for man or cause in Faneuil Hall again," O'Reilly proclaimed.

In this episode we have some measure of the burdens of Irish-American leadership. The British American Association was in the late 1880's challenging Irish political power in the city and the state. As an Irish champion, O'Reilly was obliged to oppose it, and in the process turn his back on the principles of fair play he had been preaching for a decade. To have done otherwise would have been to risk injury to Irish solidarity in hostile Boston. His difficulties are worthy of consideration by those who have been puzzled by the Irish-Catholic failure to develop a vigorous intellectual life. By far the most gifted of the leaders described in this book, he wrote his poems and novels with the Brahmins looking over one shoulder and the Irish looking over the other. No wonder that in the years before his death at forty-six his nerves failed him, and his nights were hideous with insomnia.

As Irish-American nationalism narrowed, it became more intensely Philistine. When the Dublin Abbey Players came to the United States for the first time in 1911, Devoy aroused the readers of the *Gaelic American* to attack the performances of Synge's *Playboy of the Western World* as libels on the Irish character. This, perhaps, was inevitable. The direction was fixed by Young Ireland when it set out to tame the "Wild Irish" according to English middle-class precepts. The work was continued by nationalists in the United States under the pressures of American puritanism. Even the Celtic cult, expounded by D'Arcy McGee as an alternative to American values, was soon transformed into a version of Victorianism. But philistinism was perhaps not too high a price to pay for taming the Irish. The Irishman in New York who protested the *Playboy* by throwing his watch onto the stage was a higher, if less picturesque, social type than the savage Molly Maguires of the Pennsylvania hills. If nothing else, the old passions had been diluted by prudence—the watch thrower later retrieved his possession at the stage door.

Furthermore, as Irish-American nationalism became more narcissistic, it also lost what little capacity it had had to express the full range and potentiality of Irish and American life. Present at the Abbey Theater performances in New York in 1911 was the twenty-three-year-old Eugene O'Neill. As fully Irish in his own way as Devoy, he was profoundly moved by the Irish players. They offered him a glimpse of what he might do some day. For another decade the nationalists and their organizations would remain relevant. But thereafter the future belonged to the Eugene O'Neills. Each would struggle in his own way with the trouble of being Irish.

NOTES

Chapter I

1. George Cornewall Lewis, *On Local Disturbances in Ireland* (London, 1836), p. 221. See also *Digest of Evidence Taken Before Her Majesty's Commissioners of Inquiry . . . in Respect to Occupation of Land in Ireland*, (2 vols., Dublin, 1847–48), I, p. 332.
2. Lewis, *op. cit.*, p. 131; also David Leahy, ed., *An Abstract of the Evidence Taken Before the Committee of the House of Lords Upon the State of Crime in Ireland . . . June, 1835, to January, 1839* (London, 1839), pp. 4, 10-11.
3. Quoted in Padraic Pearse, *The Spiritual Nation* . . . (Dublin, 1916), p. 11. See also *The Nation* (Dublin), February 15, 1844. For O'Connell's point of view, see his letter to Martin Crean, February 13, 1846, in W. J. Fitzpatrick, ed., *The Correspondence of Daniel O'Connell* (Dublin, 1888), II, p. 367.
4. *The Nation*, April 8, 1848.
5. *Ibid.*, January 15, 1848.
6. See the remarks of Michael Doheny in *The Nation*, February 5, 1848.
7. See *The Writings of James Fintan Lalor*, with an Introduction by John O'Leary (Dublin, 1895), *passim*.
8. Michael Doheny, *The Felon's Track* (Dublin, 1918), p. 160.
9. J. H. Whyte, *The Independent Irish Party, 1850–59* (London, 1958), especially pp. 158-177.

Chapter II

1. Batt O'Connor, *With Michael Collins in the Fight for Irish Independence* (London, 1929), p. 14.
2. John White, *Sketches From America* (London, 1870), p. 369.
3. *Irish World*, December 17, 1881.
4. Reprinted in Boston *Pilot*, September 25, 1886.
5. *Irish World*, November 13, 1880.
6. Mathew Carey, *The Olive Branch, Or Faults on Both Sides* . . . Sixth Edition, Enlarged (Philadelphia, 1815), p. 335.
7. Quoted in William Dillon, *Life of John Mitchel*, (2 vols., London, 1888), II, p. 296.

8. Oscar Handlin, "America Recognizes Diverse Loyalties," The Arden House Conference on Group Life in America (November, 1956), II, A. 32.
9. See the *American Celt*, May 7, 1853.
10. Boston *Pilot*, June 8, 22, 1878.
11. W. J. MacNeven, *Pieces of Irish History* . . . (New York, 1807), p. iii.
12. *Irish World*, September 28, 1872; also Bishop John J. Keane in Boston *Pilot*, November 24, 1888.
13. *American Celt*, January 1, 15, 1853.
14. *Irish World*, September 18, October 9, 1875; April 5, 1876.
15. *Irish Nation* (New York), April 15, 1882; also Chicago *Citizen*, August 24, 1889.
16. William D'Arcy, *The Fenian Movement in the United States 1858–1886* (Washington, D.C., 1947), p. 359.

Chapter III

1. Wayne G. Broehl, Jr., *The Molly Maguires* (Cambridge, Mass., 1964), *passim; Irish World*, June 10, 1876; June 30, 1877; Boston *Pilot*, January 19, 1878.
2. James Bryce, *The American Commonwealth*, (2 vols., 3rd edition, revised, New York, 1895), I, pp. 429 ff. For Kearney's eastern tour and the Irish reaction, see Boston *Pilot*, August 10, 24, 1878; April 18, 26, 1879; *Irish World*, August 10, 17, 31; September 14, 1878.
3. George F. Hoar, *Autobiography of Seventy Years*. (2 vols., New York, 1903), I, p. 344.
4. *Irish World*, October 21, 1876.
5. *The Congressional Record*, VII, Part V (Washington, D.C., 1878), pp. 4380-4384; *Irish World*, August 10, 1878.
6. Boston *Pilot*, October 7, 1878.
7. See the letter of Michael Scanlan, *Irish World*, October 14, 1876.
8. See the letter from "Interested," *ibid.*, May 4, 1878.
9. *Irish World*, April 5, 1879.

Chapter IV

1. *Devoy's Post Bag, 1871–1928*, William O'Brien and Desmond Ryan, editors, (2 vols., Dublin, 1948), I, pp. 288-292.
2. *Irish World*, December 4, 1875.
3. *Ibid.*, March 4, 1876.
4. See *Devoy's Post Bag*, I, p. 255-6.
5. Patrick J. P. Tynan, *The Irish National Invincibles* . . . (New York, 1894), p. 557.
6. *Northwestern Chronicle* (St. Paul), Sept. 1, 1877.
7. See Lawrence J. McCaffrey, *Irish Federalism in the 1870's: A Study*

in *Conservative Nationalism* (American Philosophical Society *Transactions*, November, 1962).

8. Joan Haslip, *Parnell: A Biography* (New York, 1937), pp. 34-37, 55; also John Howard Parnell, *Charles Stewart Parnell: A Memoir* (New York, 1914), p. 91.

9. *Irish World*, March 16, 1878.

10. Frank Hugh O'Donnell, *A History of the Irish Parliamentary Party*, (2 vols., New York, 1910), I, p. 256; also John Devoy, "Michael Davitt's Career," part XIV, *Gaelic American*, September 29, 1906.

11. In the *Gaelic American*, August 4, 1906; also *Devoy's Post Bag*, I, p. 298.

12. For varying accounts of this meeting, see *Devoy's Post Bag*, I, pp. 323-24; John Devoy, *Recollections of an Irish Rebel* (New York, 1928), p. 283; R. B. O'Brien, *Charles Stewart Parnell . . .* (2 vols., New York, 1898), I, pp. 127-8; O'Donnell, *op. cit.*, I, pp. 271-2. O'Donnell states that he was unable to win over Carroll to the support of the obstructionists. But this is contradicted by a Carroll letter to Devoy (July 20, 1878), in *Devoy's Post Bag*, I, pp. 334-336.

Chapter V

1. J. L. Garvin, *Joseph Chamberlain,* (3 vols., London, 1932), I, pp. 318-9. The best account of the New Departure's origins is to be found in T. W. Moody, "The New Departure in Irish Politics," *Essays in Honour of James Eadie Todd,* H. A. Crone, T. W. Moody, and D. B. Quinn, editors (London, 1949). Professor Moody's careful study demonstrates that the New Departure and the Land League had quite different origins, but he does not consider the positive political program of the New Departure nor its influence upon Davitt and the Land League.

2. Boston *Pilot,* June 1, 1878.

3. See Michael Davitt, *The Fall of Feudalism in Ireland* (London, 1904), pp. 111-12. There are a number of expressions of this idea. See the remarks of an "eminent M.P.," quoted in "TA's" column, *Irish World,* February 12, 1876; also Dr. Carroll to Devoy, November 16, 1877 (*Devoy's Post Bag,* I, p. 280), written just before Carroll's European journey discussed in Chapter IV. At the Dublin Home Rule convention, January, 1878, Joseph Biggar proposed withdrawing from Parliament. This proposal and Parnell's at St. Helens may have been inspired by Carroll. For Ford's endorsement, see *Irish World,* December 7, 1878.

4. See *Irish World,* October 26, 1878; also John Devoy, "Michael Davitt's Career," Part II, *Gaelic American,* June 16, 1906.

5. An *Irish World* editorial, November 23, 1878, written after the Brooklyn meeting, is suggestive. In a list of land reformers approved of by the paper no mention is made of Davitt. Devoy, however, is credited with speaking "some weeks ago, as brave and logical words as ever fell upon an Irish-American audience."

6. *Irish World,* December 7, 1878; Devoy, *Gaelic American,* September 29, 1923. Not until the issue of July 19, 1879, did Ford cease his

criticism of Parnell. By that time the threatened famine had transformed the New Departure into the land movement.

7. Boston *Pilot,* December 21, 1878; D. B. Cashman, *Life of Michael Davitt* (Boston, 1881), pp. 78-9.
8. For this evidence, see Chapter VI.
9. Michael Davitt, "Speech Delivered by Michael Davitt in Defense of the Land League" (1890), p. 2.

Chapter VI

1. See the *Irish World,* February 16, 1884, for a summary financial statement.
2. *Ibid.,* April 28, 1877; also Peter Fitzgerald, Knight of Kerry, "Mr. Froude and Irish Landlords," *Nineteenth Century,* III (1878), p. 1095.
3. *Irish World,* December 18, 1880.
4. *Ibid.,* October 23, 1880.
5. *Devoy's Post Bag,* II, pp. 21-25.
6. *Ibid.,* pp. 34-35, 70, 72-73, 91-94.
7. *Irish World,* May 7, 1881.

Chapter VII

1. *Irish World,* February 19, 1881.
2. *Ibid.,* December 11, 1880; also January 15, 22, 1881.
3. *Irish Nation* (New York), November 26, 1881.
4. *Ibid.,* December 10, 1881.
5. *Irish World,* February 11, 1882.
6. *Irish Nation,* December 24, 1881; February 11, 18, 1882; also Frederick J. Zwierlein, *The Life and Letters of Bishop McQuaid,* (3 vols., Rochester, 1926), II, pp. 274-75.
7. Michael Davitt, "The Land League Proposal: A Statement for Honest and Thoughtful Men" (Glasgow, n.d.), pp. 1-16.
8. George's letters to Ford, dated May 27 and June 8, 1882, are in the Henry George Papers, Letter Book Number 3, New York Public Library. Davitt's Liverpool speech is reprinted in part in David Bennett King, *The Irish Question* (New York, 1882), Appendix I.
9. *Irish World,* July 1, 1882.
10. *Irish Nation,* July 15, 1882.

Chapter VIII

1. For Sullivan's convention speech, see T. P. O'Connor and Robert McWade, *Gladstone-Parnell and the Great Irish Struggle* (n.p., 1886);

also, Boston *Pilot*, May 5, 1883. For Devoy's remarks, see *Irish Nation*, April 28, 1883.

2. See "Ward Thirteen," *Irish World*, December 25, 1876.
3. See the letters of Wharton Barker to Benjamin Harrison, January 30, March 1, August 6, 1888. Wharton Barker Papers, Library of Congress.
4. The vote cast for the Democratic presidential candidates in the 1880's and for Butler in 1883 and the percentages received in Boston's strong Irish wards (6, 7, 8, 12, 13) were as follows:

Hancock 1880	Butler 1883	Cleveland 1884	Cleveland 1888
7,773—79%	8,951—83%	7,485—72%	8,276—80%

5. The votes cast for the Democratic presidential candidates in the 1880's and for Hill in 1888 and the percentages received in New York's Assembly Districts 1, 2, 4, 5, 16, 18, of lower and midtown Manhattan, where the Irish were strong, were as follows:

Hancock 1880	Cleveland 1884	Cleveland 1888	Hill 1888
33,557—73%	32,113—67%	35,864—70%	39,030—77%

6. The votes cast for Cleveland in 1884 and 1888 and for Hill in 1888 and the percentages received in Brooklyn's strong Irish wards (2, 5, 6, 10, 12) were as follows:

Cleveland 1884	Cleveland 1888	Hill 1888
15,751—71%	17,028—71%	17,088—72%

Chapter IX

1. Boston *Pilot*, May 5, 1883; *Irish Nation*, May 5, 12, 1883.
2. Boston *Pilot*, March 3, July 7, 1883.
3. See the audit of the National League, *ibid.*, January 25, 1890. O'Connor and McWade, *Gladstone-Parnell and the Great Irish Struggle*, p. 749 give the receipts down to August, 1886.
4. William O'Brien, *Evening Memories* (Dublin, 1920), p. 136 ff. For a different version, see John Devoy in *Gaelic American*, September 20, 1913.
5. For a convention and its preliminaries, see Boston *Pilot*, August 21, 28; September 18, 1886; O'Connor and McWade, *op. cit.*, pp. 742-771.
6. Boston *Pilot*, April 17, 1886.
7. E. L. Godkin, "American Home Rule," and "A Lawyer's Objections to Home Rule," in *Handbook for Home Rule*, James Bryce, ed. (London, 1887).
8. See Boston *Pilot*, April 17, 1886, for a survey of American nationalist opinion of the bill.
9. See Henry George's newspaper, *The Standard*, June 4, 11, 1887.

10. The decision was reversed by a superior court and Coughlin was freed, later becoming a notorious figure in Chicago night life.
11. See Henry M. Hunt, *The Crime of the Century, or the Assassination of Dr. Patrick Henry Cronin* (Chicago, 1889), p. 376; also Chicago *Citizen,* July 13, December 21, 1889.
12. See Secretary's Report, *Fourth General Convention of the Irish National League of America* (Lincoln, Nebraska, 1891), p. 21.
13. Quoted in Emmet Larkin, "The Roman Catholic Hierarchy and The Fall of Parnell," *Publications in the Humanities,* Number 57 (Massachusetts Institute of Technology, 1962), p. 20.

A NOTE ON SOURCES

The intention of this brief note is not to list all of the sources which have been consulted in writing this book, but only those which have been of particular value. For fuller documentation of the sources the reader may consult the author's "Irish-American Nationalism, 1848-1890," unpublished doctoral dissertation, Harvard University, 1956.

Among the important manuscript collections are the George Cahill Papers and the Patrick Collins Papers, housed in the Boston College Irish Library. The Collins Papers contain important letters of the major figures—Irish and Irish-American—in the Land League movement. In the Cahill Papers we have a remarkable record of a host of minor figures active in the American nationalist movement from Fenian times down to the collapse of the National League. Included in both sets of papers are many useful documents pertaining to the Fenian Brotherhood, the Land League, and National League. The Henry George Papers in the New York Public Library are indispensable. The Margaret McKim Maloney collection in the same library includes among much valuable material a portion of the O'Donovan Rossa Papers. More of the Rossa Papers are in the archives of the Catholic University of America Library. This library also has the Terence V. Powderly Papers, which contain useful information on relations between the Knights of Labor and Clan na Gael. The Wharton Barker Papers in the Library of Congress are informative about relations between Republican party leaders and Irish-American nationalists. The single most important collection of letters for my study are the John Devoy Papers, maintained in the National Library of Ireland, which I have used in their published form: William O'Brien and Desmond Ryan, editors, *Devoy's Post Bag, 1871-1928* (2 volumes, 1948 and 1953). Helpful in appraising the influence of Irish-American nationalist activity upon Anglo-Irish relations are "Private

189

Letters from the British Embassy, 1880-1885," printed in the *Annual Report of the American Historical Association* (1942).

The Irish-American press has been the major source used for this study. In addition to the *Irish World,* the Boston *Pilot,* the Chicago *Citizen,* and John Devoy's *Nation,* much information has been drawn from the *Irish-American* of New York, edited by Patrick J. Meehan, a gossipy editor who speculated freely on the behavior of his contemporaries. John Devoy's second newspaper, the *Gaelic American,* in the decade before World War I printed fulsome obituary notices of many nationalists active in the 1880's. For the pre-Civil War period the *Truth Teller* (New York), and T. D. McGee's *Nation* and *American Celt* have been important.

Among the studies of Irish-American history Carl Wittke's *The Irish in America* (1956) and George Potter's *To the Golden Door* (1960) are informative. Potter's book, though badly organized, has much little-known information on the pre-Civil War period. *The American Irish* (1963), by William Shannon, is a brilliant book that for the first time lifts the story above the level of regret and recrimination and makes it important to American cultural history. An older but still useful book is John F. Maguire's *The Irish in America* (1868).

Of the studies in American Catholicism, I have profited from the many works of John Tracy Ellis, especially his two-volume *Life of James Cardinal Gibbons, Archbishop of Baltimore, 1834-1921* (1952). *The Emergence of Liberal Catholicism* (1958), by Robert D. Cross, is indispensable for post-Civil War Catholicism. Henry J. Browne's *The Catholic Church and the Knights of Labor* (1949), Joan Bland's *Hibernian Crusade* (1951), and J. M. Donohoe's *The Irish Catholic Benevolent Union* (1953) are excellent monographs. Aaron I. Abell's *American Catholicism and Social Action, 1865-1950* (1960) summarizes long years of study of this subject. Frederick J. Zwierlein's *The Life and Letters of Bishop McQuaid, Prefaced with The History of Catholic Rochester Before His Episcopate* (3 volumes, 1925-27) is a forthright account of an important conservative. James Moynihan's *The Life of Archbishop John Ireland* (1953) and James P. Shannon's *Catholic Colonization on the Western Frontier* (1957) are enthusiastic accounts of the work of the Archbishop of St. Paul, the central figure in Midwestern Catholicism. The latter—the best history of Catholic colonization—emphasizes the critical importance of colonization to the Catholic Midwest, even though it failed to realize the hopes of Patrick Ford and others in the East.

PROLOGUE

Good biographical studies of the major Irish-American nationalists are rare. Desmond Ryan's *The Phoenix Flame* (1937) is superficial on Devoy's life. Also disappointing in many ways is Devoy's *Recollections of an Irish Rebel* (1928). For O'Donovan Rossa, see his *Recollections* (1898) and an account by a daughter, Margaret O'Donovan Rossa, *My Mother and Father Were Irish* (1939). John Finerty lacks a biographer, but Oliver Knight's introduction to John Finerty, *War-Path and Bivouac or the Conquest of the Sioux* (1961), is helpful. Despite recent popular accounts of O'Reilly, James J. Roche's *Life of John Boyle O'Reilly, together with His Complete Poems and Speeches* (1891) remains the most useful. Arthur Mann's *Yankee Reformers in the Urban Age* (1954) contains a critical essay on O'Reilly that insufficiently appreciates his difficulties. Brief sketches of Alexander Sullivan are scattered throughout the literature of the period; the most enthusiastic of them is in T. P. O'Connor and Robert McWade's *Gladstone-Parnell and the Great Irish Struggle* (1886); the most derogatory, in Henry M. Hunt's *The Crime of the Century or the Assassination of Dr. Patrick Henry Cronin* (1889). For the life of Michael Davitt, his *Fall of Feudalism or the Story of the Land League Revolution* (1904) is a basic source. *The Life of Michael Davitt* (1881), by D. B. Cashman, imparts a sense of Davitt's early impact. M. M. O'Hara's *Chief and Tribune: Parnell and Davitt* (1919) is very suggestive on relations between the two leaders. More than most Irish writers, O'Hara considers Davitt's land nationalization ideas as important; he discusses Davitt's unhappy American tour in 1882, which Davitt ignores in the *Fall of Feudalism*. T. W. Moody, who is preparing a life of Davitt, has an excellent essay called "Michael Davitt and the British Labour Movement" in *Transactions* of the Royal Historical Society (1953), Volume III. Patrick Ford apparently destroyed most of his papers and material on his life is scarce. See the sketch in the *Dictionary of American Biography* (1937) Volume VI; the interesting portrayal in *Twenty Five Years in the Secret Service: The Recollections of a Spy* (1892) by Major

Henri Le Caron (Thomas Miller Beach); and the sketch by a British journalist, reprinted in the Boston *Pilot*, Sept. 25, 1886.

CHAPTER I

Fuller treatment and documentation of many points raised in this chapter is given in the author's "Nationalism and the Irish Peasant," *Review of Politics* (1953), Volume XV. K. H. Connell's *The Population of Ireland, 1750-1845* (1950) is authoritative and corrects old errors. To the traditional liberal and nationalist history of the eighteenth-century, Robert E. Burns offers important revisions in "The Irish Penal Code and Some of its Historians," and "The Belfast Letters, the Irish Volunteers, and the Catholics," *Review of Politics* (1959) Volume XXI. Voluminous material on Whiteboyism is available in the many investigations of rural crime carried out by special committees of the House of Lords and Commons and by royal commissions. Some of those which I have examined are cited in the footnotes. The writer William Carleton (1794-1869) is the best historian of the peasantry. Thomas Flanagan's *The Irish Novelists, 1800-1850* (1959) has a discriminating account of his work. A recent book by Wayne Broehl, *The Molly Maguires* (1964), is sensible on the peasant secret societies. Two excellent works on the Famine are *The Great Famine* (1957), R. Dudley Edwards and T. Desmond Williams, editors, and Cecil Woodham-Smith's *The Great Hunger* (1962). Though very different in tone, both conclude that British failures in the crisis were the results of ineptitude and *laissez faire* idolatry rather than maliciousness, as the Irish had thought. I am particularly indebted to Keven B. Nowlan's "The Political Background" in *The Great Famine* for its careful analysis of relations between O'Connell and Young Ireland. Denis Gwynn's *Daniel O'Connell, the Liberator* (1947), and Sean O'Faolain's *King of the Beggars* (1938) are contrasting studies of O'Connell. The latter is rich in insight. Also of importance is *Daniel O'Connell: Nine Centenary Essays* (1949), Michael Tierney, editor. James A. Reynolds's *The Catholic Emancipation Crisis in Ireland, 1823-1829* (1954) is good but insufficiently discriminating on peasant support. Nothing comparable to it exists for the Repeal movement. For this, the Young Ireland newspaper *The Nation* is basic. The various reports of the Loyal National Repeal Association, Dublin

(1845) are helpful. Despite their exaggeration of Young Ireland's differences with O'Connell, the works of Charles Gavan Duffy remain important: *Young Ireland: A Fragment of Irish History* (1881), *Four Years of Irish History* (1883), and *Thomas Davis* (1890). Michael Tierney's "Thomas Davis: 1814-1845" and "Nationalism: A Survey," *Studies*, Dublin (1945), Volume XXXIV are suggestive on the European influence. Denis Gwynn's *Young Ireland and 1848* (1949) includes narratives by a number of participants in the insurrection. J. H. Whyte's *The Independent Irish Party, 1850-9* (1958) corrects the traditional view of the Tenant Right movement and the Irish Parliamentary Party of the 1850's.

CHAPTER II

This chapter is a revised statement of the author's "The Origins and Character of Irish-American Nationalism," *Review of Politics* (1956), Volume XVIII, which the reader should consult for fuller documentation of the points raised. This analysis of the Irish-American community's formation is deeply indebted to Oscar Handlin's classic study *Boston's Immigrants: A Study in Acculturation*, Revised and Enlarged (1959). For materials on Irish emigration I have drawn on the Irish Government's "Commission on Emigration and Other Population Problems, 1948-54," Mimeographed (n.d.), which contains a number of useful historical tables; Brinley Thomas's *Migration and Economic Growth* (1954); Stanley C. Johnson's *A History of Emigration from the United Kingdom to North America, 1763-1912* (1912); Oliver MacDonagh's "Irish Emigration to the United States of America and the British Colonies During the Famine," in *The Great Famine*, Edwards and Williams, editors; and Cecil Woodham-Smith's *The Great Hunger*. Arnold Schrier's *Ireland and the American Emigration* (1958) offers an analysis of the social and geographical sources of Irish emigration. Woodham-Smith's *The Great Hunger*, Handlin's *Boston's Immigrants*, and Robert Ernst's *Immigrant Life in New York City, 1825-1863* (1949) deal with the circumstances of pre-Civil War immigrant life. E. P. Hutchinson's *Immigrants and Their Children, 1850-1950* (1956) shows the relatively slow rise of the Irish into the middle classes.

The *Truth Teller*, edited in New York by Major William Denman, reflects the relative ease of the American Irish before the Famine. McGee's *Nation* and *Celt* in contrast mirror great tension. Potter's *To the Golden Door* is rich in ill-assimilated information dealing with the period. Deasmun O Raghallaigh, "William James MacNeven," *Studies*, Dublin (1941), Volume XXX is useful. Mathew Carey's reminiscences, which first appeared in 1833-34, have been collected in his *Autobiography* (1942). Carey's own voluminous pamphlet literature and Earl J. Bradsher's *Mathew Carey, Editor, Author, Publisher* (1912) are helpful. Isabel Skelton's *The Life of Thomas D'Arcy McGee* (1925) is excellent. William Dillon's *Life of John Mitchel*, (2 vols., 1888) contains generous extracts from Mitchel's correspondence.

Most of the material on the Celt and language movement is drawn from the immigrant press. Desmond Ryan's *The Sword of Light* (1939) surveys the language movement in Ireland. For early antiquarian interest, see Edward Reilly's preface to *Transactions of the Iberno-Celtic Society for 1820*, Part I, Dublin (1820). A more militant spirit can be observed in John O'Mahoney's comments in his translation of Geoffrey Keating's *The History of Ireland . . .* (1857). Edward N. Saveth's *American Historians and European Immigrants* (1948) is good on American historians and the Anglo-Saxon myth. John V. Kelleher's "Matthew Arnold and the Celtic Revival," in *Perspectives of Criticism* (1950), edited by Harry Levin, is excellent on Arnold's dubious influence. Representative expressions of the clerical view of Irish history are August J. Thebaud's *Ireland: Past and Present . . .* (1878), and J. L. Spalding's *The Religious Mission of the Irish People and Catholic Colonization* (1880). An extreme but not unrepresentative national view of Irish history is James G. McGuire's *Ireland and the Pope: A Brief History of Papal Intrigues Against Irish Liberty . . .* (1888).

On the American Fenian movement I have followed William D'Arcy's *The Fenian Movement in the United States, 1858-1886* (1947), which makes good use of the Rossa Papers at Catholic University. John Savage's *Fenian Heroes and Martyrs* (1868) emphasizes the Americanization of the movement. John Devoy's *Recollections . . .* (1928), Mark Ryan, *Fenian Memories* (1945), and John O'Leary's *Recollections of Fenians and Fenianism* (1896) are among the best of the memoirs.

CHAPTER III

In addition to the *Irish World*, whose pages offer a good chronicle of the Greenback movement in the 1870's, I have drawn upon Chester M. Destler's *American Radicalism, 1865-1890* (1946). *The History of American Labour* (1922), Volume II, by John R. Commons and Associates, is useful on greenback theory. T. Ainge Devyr's *The Odd Book of the Nineteenth Century* . . . (1882), by an *Irish World* staff member and old-time land reformer, helps to relate Ford to pre-Civil War reformers. George E. McNeill's *The Labor Movement* (1887) has much obscure information on the labor situation in Massachusetts. Frank Roney's *Irish Rebel and California Labor Leader: An Autobiography*, edited by Ira B. Cross, (1931) is good on Kearney's activities. "Some Denominational Reactions to Chinese Immigration to California, 1865-1892," *Pacific Historical Review* (1959), Volume XXVIII by Robert Seager II, describes the religious aspects of Kearneyism. Butler's biographers show little interest in the latter stages of his career. The *Pilot* and the considerable pamphlet literature that Butler aroused his Massachusetts' friends and enemies to write are important sources. A. P. Stauffer's "Anti-Catholicism in American Politics, 1865-1900," unpublished doctoral dissertation, Harvard University, is helpful on the Irish emergence in Massachusetts politics. M. P. Curran's *The Life of Patrick Collins* (1906) has much on Butler's relations with the regular Democrats. Solomon Bulkley Griffin's *On People and Politics* (1923) is another account by a contemporary. The best biography is Hans J. Trefusse's *Ben Butler: The South Called Him Beast* (1957). The Irish landlord system in the 1870's is discussed in Norman D. Palmer's *The Irish Land League Crisis* (1940). Fergus McDonald's *The Catholic Church and Secret Societies in the United States* (1946) deals chiefly with the ecclesiastical side of the problem.

CHAPTER IV

On Fenianism in the 1870's and the foundation of the Clan na Gael, I have drawn on D'arcy's *The Fenian Movement*, the instructive comments by the editors of *Devoy's Post Bag*, and Le Caron's *Twenty Five Years in the Secret Service*. H. B. C. Pollard's *The Secret Societies of Ireland* (1922), an otherwise unreliable book reprints the Clan na Gael constitution. Z. W. Pease's *The Catalpa Expedition* (1897) tells the story of the rescue mission to Australia. Lawrence McCaffrey's "Irish Federalism in the 1870's: A Study in Conservative Nationalism," American Philosophical Society *Transactions* (1962), Volume 52 is a careful and thoughtful analysis that corrects earlier interpretations of Butt's Home Rule movement. Also helpful are Terence De Vere White's *The Road of Excess* (1945), a biography of Butt, and Michael McDonagh's *The Home Rule Movement* (1920), which draws upon the papers of John O'Connor Power. Frank Hugh O'Donnell's two volumes, *A History of the Irish Parliamentary Party* (1910) is malicious and self-serving but tells much about the rivalry with Parnell. The first volume of Timothy Healy's, *Letters and Leaders of My Day* (1929) is also useful in this respect. T. P. O'Connor's *The Parnell Movement* (1886) provides an anecdotal account of the Obstructionists. R. Barry O'Brien's *The Life of Charles Stewart Parnell*, (2 vols., 1899) remains the best general biography but is outdated in many particulars. Conor Cruise O'Brien's *Parnell and His Party* (1957) is a brilliant book which emphasizes Parnell's prudence and the political usefulness of his famed eccentricity. I am under great obligation to this work.

CHAPTER V

Any study of the New Departure must begin with T. W. Moody's "The New Departure in Irish Politics," *Essays in British and Irish History in Honour of James Eadie Todd,* edited by T. W. Moody, H. A. Crone, and D. B. Quinn, (1949). In extending Professor Moody's work, I have depended chiefly on a close reading of the Irish-American press for the period 1877-1882, when the New Departure plan was formulated and aborted, and later when Davitt's interpretation was repeatedly challenged. The relevant letters in Devoy's *Post Bag*, Volume I, are of the greatest importance in finding one's way through the maze of contradictory assertions made by the participants in the New Departure's original program. On the whole Devoy's accounts in the *Land of Eire* (1882) and in the *Gaelic American,* June through November, 1906, stand up well. Davitt's account in the *Fall of Feudalism* is ambiguous, to say the least; so are his testimony and speech before the Special Commission (The *Times, Parnellism and Crime: The Special Commission,* Parts XXVII, XXXI). Traditional accounts, such as in Palmer's *Land League Crisis,* and L. P. Curtis's

Coercion and Conciliation in Ireland, 1880-1892 . . . (1963), which identify the New Departure with the Land League and make Davitt the hero of both, are wide of the mark.

CHAPTERS VI and VII

Palmer's *Land League Crisis*, remains the best general survey of the land struggle between 1878 and 1882, though it is deficient in understanding of the political and social forces that shaped the Land League's history, partly because of its defective grasp of the New Departure. The Collins Papers are indispensable for relations between the American and Irish leagues; the Henry George Papers, for the Parnell-Davitt conflict in 1882. James J. Greene's "American Catholics and the Irish Land League," *Catholic Historical Review* (1949), Volume XXXV is a good survey. Kenneth E. Colton's "Parnell's Mission to Iowa," *Annals of Iowa* (1940), Volume XXII describes Parnell's success in one state. Philip H. Bagenal's *The American Irish and Their Influence on Irish Politics* (1882) and "Uncle Pat's Cabin," *Nineteenth Century* (1882), Volume XII are works of insight by a contemporary. The first deals with the Irish-American factions; the second, with the agricultural laborers' demands upon the tenant farmers in the League. Zwierlein's *Life of Bishop McQuaid*, tells of Bishop Gilmour's troubles. Charles A. Barker's *Henry George* (1955) is excellent. *The Life of Henry George* (1900) by Henry George, Jr., is useful on Davitt's 1882 tour. O'Brien, *Parnell and His Party*, carefully charts the course of Parnell and rejects the probability of his seriously considering implementing the New Departure's revolutionary proposals.

On the subsidiary question of when Davitt was converted to land nationalization, M. M. O'Hara's *Chief and Tribune: Parnell and Davitt* (1919) appears to believe that Davitt emerged from prison in 1877 with such ideas and that he met Henry George as early as 1878, while on his first American tour. I am grateful to Professor Owen Edwards of the University of Oregon for directing me to Andrew J. Kettle's *The Material for Victory; Being the Memoir of Andrew J. Kettle*, edited by L. J. Kettle, (1958), which makes a similar point. The weight of the evidence, however, is against this contention.

CHAPTER VIII

Oscar Handlin's *The Uprooted* (1951), has a keen apprecia-
tion of the significance of politics for the Irish. See also his "The
Immigrant in American Politics," *Foreign Influences in American
Life,* edited by D. F. Bowers, (1952). Daniel Moynihan's "The Irish,"
in *Beyond the Melting Pot* (1963), by Daniel Moynihan and Nathan
Glazer, is illuminating on Irish-American political behavior but is too
insistent on tracing its origins to Ireland. Irish politicians like Tim
Healy were as impressed as native Americans by Irish-American man-
agerial qualities. Florence Gibson's *The Attitudes of the New York
Irish Toward State and National Affairs, 1848-92* (1951) contains
much valuable information but suffers from the conviction that Irish-
Americans had no right to their own political interests and style. Allan
Nevins's *Grover Cleveland: A Study in Courage* (1932) and Denis T.
Lynch's *Grover Cleveland: A Man Four Square* (1932) suffer from
the same disability. *Benjamin Harrison: Hoosier Statesman,* (1959),
volume 2 by Harry J. Sievers, S.J., offers good, if traditional, summa-
ries of the 1884 and 1888 elections. Herbert Bass's *I Am a Democrat:
The Political Career of David Bennett Hill* (1961) is good. Gordon S.
Wood's "The Massachusetts Mugwumps," *New England Quarterly*
(1960), Volume XXXIII, points out the circumstances which shaped
Collins's loyalty to Cleveland. In the election of 1886, I have supplemented Barker's *George,* with "The George-Hewitt Campaign of
1886," (n.d.), by Louis F. Post and F. C. Leubuscher, and P. A.
Speek's "The Single Tax and the Labor Movement," *Bulletin* of the
University of Wisconsin (1914-18), Volume VIII. The Henry George
Papers are thin for the elections of 1886 and 1887, but the *Standard*
for 1887 is a valuable source for George's activities that year. Edward
McGlynn's "The New Know Nothingism and the Old," *North American Review,* (1887-8), Volume CXLV is angry and typical of what
alienated Irish Catholics. F. J. Zwierlein's *Letters of Archbishop Cor-
rigan to Bishop McQuaid and Allied Documents* (1946) deals with
Corrigan's handling of the McGlynn situation.

The distribution of the Irish by wards in Boston for the purpose of
election analysis was derived from C. D. Wright's *The Census of
Massachusetts: 1880* (1883); the distribution in Brooklyn wards,
from C. W. Seaton's *The Census of the State of New York for 1875*

(1877). Since New York election returns were by Assembly and Election Districts, not by wards, Seaton's figures were not relevant. I chose therefore the Assembly Districts of Midtown and Lower Manhattan which traditionally gave Tammany its greatest majorities. New York election figures for 1880 and 1884 are compiled from New York City, *The City Record, Official Journal,* supplements for November, 1880, and December, 1884. The figures for 1888 are from the New York *Times,* November 8, 1888. Brooklyn returns are from the Boston *Globe,* November 7, 1888, New York *Times,* November 8, 1888. Boston's vote is compiled from Boston *Herald,* November 7, 1883, November 7, 1888; Boston *Advertiser* and Boston *Globe,* November 5, 1884.

CHAPTER IX

Useful, if not always accurate, accounts of the Clan na Gael, the Dynamite Campaign, and the American National League are in Sir Henry James's *The Work of the Irish Leagues* (1890), which summarizes the London *Times* charges against Parnell and his followers before the Special Commission, and Sir Charles Russell's *The Parnell Commission: The Opening Speech for the Defense* (1889). James insists, quite erroneously, that the American League was simply a front organization for the Clan but he rightly notes the degree to which the Clan had infiltrated the leadership. Le Caron's testimony in *Twenty Five Years in the Secret Service* is important and in many particulars, persuasive. Hunt's *The Crime of the Century,* bases his narrative of the dynamite campaign chiefly on the testimony offered at the Cronin trial. John T. McEnnis's *The Clan na Gael and the Murder of Dr. Patrick Henry Cronin* (1889) is the most useful book on this matter. Sir Robert Anderson's *Sidelights on the Home Rule Movement* (1906) is an account by the Assistant Commissioner of Police, who handled Le Caron's reports.

O'Brien's *Parnell and His Party,* and Curtis's *Coercion and Conciliation,* tell the complex story of the Home Rule party's relations with British Liberals and Conservatives. Michael Davitt's, "The Report of the Parnell Commission," *Nineteenth Century* (1890), Volume XXVII disputes the Parnell Commission report and testifies to the moderating influence of Parnell's leadership upon the Irish-Americans. *Gladstone-*

Parnell and the Great Irish Struggle, by O'Connor and McWade, offers useful biographical sketches of prominent figures in the American League. Richard C. Murphy's *The Society of the Friendly Sons of St. Patrick in the City of New York, 1784-1955* (1962), and John E. Campbell's *History of the Friendly Sons of St. Patrick and of the Hibernian Society* . . . , *1771-1892* (1892), provide a wealth of ill-organized information on the wealthy Irish of New York and Philadelphia respectively. "The Use of the American Civil War in the Debate Over Irish Home Rule," by J. M. Hernon, Jr., in *American Historical Review*, (1964), Volume LXIX is short but helpful.

INDEX